A Sensory History Manifesto

## Perspectives on Sensory History

Books in the Perspectives on Sensory History series
maintain a historical basis for work on the senses,
examining how the experiences of seeing, hearing,
smelling, tasting, and touching have shaped the ways
in which people have understood their worlds.

# A Sensory History
# Manifesto

Mark M. Smith

The Pennsylvania State University Press
University Park, Pennsylvania

Library of Congress Cataloging-in-
    Publication Data

Names: Smith, Mark M. (Mark Michael),
    1968– author.
Title: A sensory history manifesto / Mark
    M. Smith.
Other titles: Perspectives on sensory history.
Description: University Park, Pennsylvania :
    The Pennsylvania State University Press,
    [2021] | Series: Perspectives on sensory
    history | Includes bibliographical
    references and index.
Summary: "An exploration of the past,
    present, and future of sensory history"—
    Provided by publisher.
Identifiers: LCCN 2021012401 | ISBN
    9780271090177 (hardback) | ISBN
    9780271090184 (paperback)
Subjects: LCSH: Senses and
    sensation—History.
Classification: LCC BF233 .S55 2021 | DDC
    152.1—dc23
LC record available at https://lccn.loc.gov
    /2021012401

# Contents

# Acknowledgments

Some of the central points I make in this book have been tested at a variety of conferences and lectures, and I remain deeply grateful for the comments offered on those occasions. Especially rewarding were conversations resulting from my presentations on various aspects of sensory history at the Music and Culture Colloquium Series, University of South Carolina, Columbia, SC, February 14, 2020; the Department of History, University of Adelaide, Australia, May 3, 2019; the Centre for Interdisciplinary Studies in Society and Culture, Concordia University, Montreal, Quebec, Canada, October 5, 2017; the Danish National Archives, Copenhagen, Denmark, June 10, 2017; the Vanderbilt History Seminar, Vanderbilt University, Nashville, TN, April 10, 2017; the London Jazz Festival, London, UK, November 17, 2016; the meeting of the Austrian American Studies Association, University of Graz, Graz, Austria, November 7, 2015; and the Department of History, Queens University of Charlotte, Charlotte, NC, October 3, 2015. For their careful reading of the manuscript and their guidance, I wish to thank David Howes (Concordia University, Montreal, Canada), Peter Denney (Griffith University, Brisbane, Australia), and Tim Lockley (University of Warwick, UK). Sincere thanks, also, to Lesa Scholl for inviting me to speak on the book at Kathleen Lumley College, Adelaide, Australia, in 2019 and for listening to my thinking. I remain grateful to Ed Linenthal and my colleague, Paul MacKenzie, for discussing aspects of this book with me and for sharing helpful leads. Kendra Boileau, Editor-in-Chief at Penn State University Press, has been dogged in her support of this book, and she has my enduring thanks.

# Introduction

Consider this short book an engaged meditation on the state of the "field" (more properly, "habit" or methodology) of sensory history.[1] It is primarily concerned with how historians of the senses engage with and write about the subject. It begins from the premise—one accepted by sensory historians generally—that, as sensory anthropologist David Howes puts it, "the sensorium is a historical formation."[2] How historians have written about those formations, what (and how) they are currently writing about them, and what (and how) they might be writing about in future years constitute the underpinnings of this short study.

This is in no way a catholic survey of recent and ongoing work; instead, it is an attempt to offer a modest manifesto. It is at once a call and an invitation: a cordial invitation to historians who are unfamiliar with sensory history to adopt some of its insights and practices, and a gentle call to current practitioners to think in new ways about writing histories of the senses. The book ponders three interconnected issues. First, it traces what we might think of as some of the origins of historical work on the senses, long before the emergence of the nomenclature of "sensory history." It interrogates, explores, and, in some cases, recovers some important and arguably pioneering work on the senses that has been forgotten or slighted in more recent treatments. The purpose of recovering—and engaging with—this historiographical genealogy is twofold. First, it is born of my own conviction that few innovations in any field of historical writing are wholly original and that we are under a professional obligation to at least acknowledge foundational work. Second, and more importantly, I remain convinced that if the current state of writing on the history of the senses is to evolve, refine, and emerge as more interpretively powerful, we would be well advised to consult, with care, some of the earliest work on the senses. As chapter 1 shows in some detail, the strengths and weaknesses of this early work can be understood profitably by current scholars of the senses. Early work both reveals the pitfalls of writing about past senses—including missteps that still inflect some writing today—and alerts us to possible new directions in sensory history. While this work did not always fully develop these new directions, early practitioners thought carefully enough about what they were doing to allow us to pivot from their foundational insights to offer additional ways of writing about and researching the senses. It is also worth noting that early work reflected an interpretive divide on how to write, historically, about the senses; it is a divide that still has some resonance today, and reading these early works with care helps us move beyond it.

We are at an important moment in the writing of sensory history. As I document in chapter 2, it is expanding rapidly, even though it is not as new as some observers sometimes seem to think. Here, I explain the potential that sensory history holds for the study of history generally—why, in other words, the discipline of historical writing should take the senses seriously. I offer examples, including a quite detailed illustration, not only of how sensory history expands our understanding of the past but of how its exclusion leaves us impoverished. This part of the book is an invitation to the historical profession generally to take seriously the senses and it showcases some work in an effort to incentivize that embrace.

In chapter 3, I highlight the strengths of the current iteration of sensory history and identify some of its shortcomings. Unless sensory history thinks carefully about its future, it courts the real possibility of deadening its interpretive power and slipping into quiet desuetude. If sensory history offers historians of all persuasions, times, and places a real, useful, and incisive way to write about the past, it also challenges current practitioners to attend to the historicity of the senses and the desirability—even the urgency—of engaged and sustained debate among themselves. In the third chapter, I ponder what, collectively, historians of the senses are doing with their field and suggest what else they could be doing with it. I am happy to disclose that I have been banging this drum for a couple of decades in various ways. I do so again now because while I am quite thrilled with (and, in very small part, responsible for) some of the work being produced by historians of the senses, I am concerned that without the sort of intervention I am calling for, the field will become etiolated.[3] I invite current practitioners to think about how their "field" probably needs to evolve if the real interpretive dividends of sensory history are to be realized, to think about initiatives that will help the field flourish profitably and avoid lapsing into a kind of comfortable comradery that, while valuable in many ways, can unintentionally deprive us of the dialectic necessary for robust interpretive growth. Sensory history will have done its work when its habit, the incorporation of the sensate into our understanding of the past, has assumed a naturalized quality so that historical writing generally attends to all of the senses in some fashion. At that point, sensory history will no longer be a stand-alone habit or field. Put simply, attention to the senses will be part and parcel of a historical sensibility. Until that point, sensory historians must attend to some important matters and think carefully about their own work.

Part of this call—a challenge to us all, myself included—is born of my own particular research interests. Most of it is a product of my reading of recent literature and reviews, some of which hint at a growing unease with simply celebrating sensory history as "new" and "burgeoning" and a desire to more actively critique the work that is being produced in a way that simultaneously encourages the production of more scholarship but also considers the core methodological and interpretive issues underwriting sensory history. In other words, for sensory history—as a way to "do" history, as a habit of historical inquiry—to inflect mainstream historical writing, current tensions in the field require attention and resolution. Until those tensions are addressed, historians generally will remain—wisely—dubious about the benefits of sensory history.

The third aim of this essay—also outlined in chapter 3—is, simply, not only to suggest how sensory history should be written and researched but to identify a number of topics that could profitably be examined through the senses. Some of my suggestions here are based on work I know to be ongoing and forthcoming; others reflect my own particular interests for the field; still others are hopeful suggestions. Plainly, I do not want readers to think I offer anything exhaustive here.

This book makes no pretense of offering original empirical research. Rather, it is based on my reading of the field as a whole, my main conclusions derived from what has been written and what is currently being written about the history of the senses. Certainly, what I offer here is by no means an exhaustive survey. Such an undertaking is not only beyond the scope of a short book—the sheer volume of material already published on sensory history is daunting—but unnecessary. The principal lines of inquiry, fissures of debate, and main trajectories in the field are discernable in general terms and accessible in summary form.

Lastly, I need to point out that this book is not a critique of sensory studies generally. It is not especially concerned with, for example, how the disciplines of anthropology and sociology are wrestling with the sensate. Such a treatment is readily available elsewhere. That much said, and as will become apparent, I am very much of the opinion that future writing on the history of the senses will benefit enormously from further interdisciplinary engagement.[4]

# CHAPTER 1

# Past

## Gestures

While welcome, the sheer number of books and articles published on the history of the senses, especially in the past two decades—its very speed and reach—has sometimes occluded the important and much earlier work done by historians on the topic. We tend, wrongly, to think of sensory history as terribly new. It is not. As Michele Hilmes helpfully observed in 2005, the field of sound studies, for example, has been described as "emerging" for decades.[1] While this is probably truer of sound studies than for the other, nonvisual senses, there is, nonetheless, a deeper genealogy of historical work on the senses than is often recognized.

At some level, it is arguably foolhardy to talk about a generalized "sensory history," not least because there is too much asymmetry and unevenness in historical writing on the senses.

We have a great deal of work on the history of seeing and look-ing, and the history of vision has the deepest genealogy and most robust historiography of any of the senses.[2] Work on the histories of hearing, listening, sound, and noise far outnumber, combined, the number of books and articles published to date on histories of smell, taste, and touch. And, despite a couple of seminal books, work on touch and taste is easily overshadowed, in terms of quantity, by writing on olfaction. Still, given his-torians' increasing interest in the senses, it seems appropriate to think about the field of sensory history as having arrived. After all, a growing number of studies treat multiple senses, and even those that light on one sense often frame their work within the history of multiple senses. The point I wish to stress here is that sensory history, while uneven, not only exists but has existed for quite some time. I wish to highlight the exis-tence of early work on the history of the senses not simply to nod to the fact that historiography matters (although I believe it does) and not to make claims about the "origins" of sensory history (something of a fruitless task). Rather, I wish to point to and take stock of this early work not least because it offers useful guidance to historians today, even if it is not much read or cited. Few historians have acknowledged, let alone explored, these distant origins, and the oversight is a shame.[3] Reading (and rereading) this work helps us appreciate the innovativeness of historians working on the senses long before there was some-thing thought of as the field of sensory history; it also helps us confront and go some way toward resolving interpretive prob-lems apparent in the current historiography. This is not to say these earlier writers were wholly correct. Nor is it some nos-talgic call for their veneration. Some of what they wrote about the senses and perception was muddled and poorly conceptual-ized. But enough of what these historians wrote was insightful and is worth paying attention to today.

This chapter outlines some of these early influences. By "early," I mean pre-twenty-first-century historians. And by historians I do not mean those, such as Karl Marx, who simply referred to the senses occasionally (albeit powerfully). Instead, I am interested in more sustained treatments demonstrating how early historians thought about the senses and how they wrote about them. They did not necessarily refer to "sensory history," but some of them talked meaningfully about "historical sensation" and the senses. I suggest that the two main ways sensory historians have, up until quite recently, approached the senses—as either highly contextualized historically or as highly decontextualized phenomena, capable of reproduction from the vantage point of the present and quite transferable between the "us" of now and the "them" of the past—were apparent in the early work of sensory historians.[4]

We begin with the influential Dutch historian Johan Huizinga (1872–1945), who wrote, if not extensively then certainly meaningfully, about the presence and role of the senses in the past and offered thoughts on how historians might best go about approaching them. As one of the founders of modern cultural history, Huizinga brought to bear a concern with recognizing the importance of "historical sensation," particularly in the Middle Ages and Renaissance.[5]

As Frank Ankersmit has persuasively argued, Huizinga's attempts to engage sensation, particularly in his influential 1919 work, *Herfsttij der Middeleeuwen: Studie Over Levens-en-Gedachtenvormen der Veertiende en Vijftiende Eeuw in Frankrijk en de Nederlanden* (translated as *The Autumn of the Middle Ages* or *The Waning of the Middle Ages*), were born of his training as a linguist and, as such, he was an early practitioner of interdisciplinarity. According to Ankersmit, Huizinga tried to move beyond simply conveying historical "experience" to capturing "historical sensation" but did so in ways that compromised the

importance of historical context in anchoring sensory understanding and meaning. Huizinga's historical methodology was
deliberately on the side of decontextualization, and his interest
in historical sensation played an important role in shaping that
phenomenology and posture. Huizinga's understanding of historical experience, in which historical sensation plays an important part, occurs, writes Ankersmit, when all "spatial and temporal
demarcations have momentarily been lifted; it is as if the temporal trajectory between past and present, instead of separating the
two, has become the locus of their encounter. Historical experience pulls the faces of past and present together in a short but
ecstatic kiss." Nonvisual phenomena especially appealed to Huizinga because he believed they held an authenticity, with sounds
granting deeper understanding of the human condition than that
offered by sight alone. Huizinga found something immediate,
even emotional, in studying how people in the past sensed, and
Ankersmit contends that Huizinga believed that a direct confron-
tation with the sensory past yielded the most authentic evidence
to the historian, one that placed the senses and emotion into
direct dialogue. Here, Huizinga's penchant for "decontextualization" mattered tremendously. As Ankersmit puts it, "historical
experience and contextualization mutually exclude each other,"
allowing us, in Huizinga's opinion, to strip away the muddying
gauze of historiography and accreted interpretations. In turn, this
allows for a sort of pure access to the sensory experience of the
past that, in Huizinga's telling, is also the sensory experience of
the present. The bridge for translating "the sound or the smell
of the past" into historical text was language. Interested in the
sensitivist movement with its emphasis on feeling and trained
as a linguist, Huizinga, in some of his historical writing, appears
preoccupied with "the problem of translating the data of (sensory) experience into language." We see this most clearly, says
Ankersmit, in *The Waning of the Middle Ages*.[6]

There is not much doubt that the sensory—especially sight and sound—was important to Huizinga. By only the second page in *The Waning of the Middle Ages*, we are introduced to the medieval European town visually and auditorily. Fascinatingly, Huizinga makes a case, albeit briefly, for how the era and its underlying culture affected the ratio of the senses, thereby anticipating a key observation by Marshall McLuhan and Walter Ong by a few decades. "The contrast between silence and sound, darkness and light, like that between summer and winter, was more strongly marked than it is in our lives," writes Huizinga, elaborating: "The modern town hardly knows silence or darkness in their purity, nor the effect of a solitary light or a single distant cry." Now, there's a lot wrong with this claim, of course. Huizinga documents none of it; he elides and flattens a complex cultural and social topography, treating everyone in the past as one, undifferentiated sensory clump. The idea that sound and sight existed with some sort of unmediated "purity" while moderns exist in a mucky, compromised sensory state only serves to reinscribe the conceit of the distant past as somehow sensorially untinctured. The sensory historian should be interested not only in the specificity of that claim but, more especially, in the ways in which people in the past understood this putative purity, if, in fact, they perceived in that way at all. Still, Huizinga is nodding toward an essential fact: the senses existed in the past and are worthy of study.[7]

Huizinga anticipates much in later sensory historical writing. He gestures to Alain Corbin's canonically important work on the significance of bells (which I discuss later). Using uncomfortably broad (but quite seductive) brushstrokes, Huizinga paints a soundscape of the urban Middle Ages. His words are worth quoting not least because he shows how historians can—and have—used literary devices to try to capture the role of the senses in animating the past. Writes Huizinga: "One sound rose ceaselessly above the noises of busy life and lifted all things unto a sphere of order and serenity: the sound of bells. The bells were in daily life like good spirits, which by their familiar voices, now called upon the citizens to mourn and now to rejoice, now warned them of danger, now exhorted them to piety." Here, the Dutch historian appeals to only the very broadest context to capture the feel or atmosphere of an age; he is far less interested in delineating how particular groups heard and how habits of hearing changed over time and varied among constituencies. He makes claims that, while fascinating, are wholly unsupported: "However continuous the ringing of the bells, people would seem not to have become blunted to the effect of their sound." Still, Huizinga does important architectural work here by weaving sounds and explicit acts and habits of seeing into the very tapestry of his narrative. It is especially noteworthy that Huizinga braids emotion and the sensate: sounds held the capacity to inspire sadness and happiness, for example. Historians of the senses would do well to ponder this association in much greater detail.[8]

Rich, heavily textured, and often brilliant prose was the conduit for Huizinga's attempts to translate historical sensation into language. *The Waning of the Middle Ages* is written always with the present in mind and deploys evocative prose to capture the sensation and the feel of the late Burgundian Middle Ages. Huizinga, at least according to Ankersmit (with whom I am inclined to agree), uses language to conflate the past and present when detailing sensations. "When writing this book," says Huizinga, "it was as if my gaze was directed into the depths of an evening sky—but a sky full of a bloody red and angry with a threatening lead-grey, full of a false copper shine." This is how Huizinga captured the feel, the sensation, the atmosphere of the era. This was sensory history, Huizinga style.[9]

Judging by Huizinga's most explicit statements concerning the nature of historical methodology, which he wrote later, his

willingness to approach the history of sensation in such decontextualized form is not particularly consistent with his sense of
how to go about writing history. In his influential 1929 essay,
"The Task of Cultural History," he argued that shoddy historical writing occurs when "the mind selects from tradition certain elements it synthesizes into a historically coherent image,
which was not realized in the past as it was lived." "The past
as it was lived" is the key phrase and suggests that Huizinga
thought that context was essential to writing reliable history.[10]
So why did Huizinga suspend his own rules when it came to
writing about historical sensory sensations? I think part of the
answer has to do with what I think of as the seduction of the
senses; sensorial language can lure even careful historians into
collapsing the distance between present and past. As we shall
see, that temptation, albeit for additional reasons, lives on in
some historical writing.

Huizinga's brushstrokes were necessary but insufficient
to establish anything resembling a workable sensory history.
For that foundation to be properly established, momentum and
refinement were needed. This came from a variety of scholars,
sometimes working in relative isolation, preeminently among
them Lucien Febvre, Robert Mandrou, Guy Thuillier, and Oscar
Handlin.[11]

## Growth

Lucien Febvre (1878–1956) is a towering figure among historians in the twentieth century. A close friend of Marc Bloch
(1886–1944), Febvre was a cofounder of the *Annales* School. In
1929, they established *Annales d'histoire économique et sociale*,
a journal promoting the study of highly contextualized social
history, framed around the idea of the *longue durée* and deeply

committed to understanding the *mentalité* of people in the past. Febvre and Bloch and the entire school of *Annalistes* were much less interested in political and diplomatic history than they were in unearthing the attitudes, culture, and beliefs of people in the past and relating them to the social and economic context in which they existed.[12]

It is not in the writings of Bloch or, indeed, even Fernand Braudel (1902–1985), the other most influential *Annaliste*, that we find sustained reference to the senses but, rather, in Febvre. It seems fitting to focus on Febvre's most extensive commentary on the senses, which we find in his *Le problème de l'incroyance au XVI^e siècle: La religion de Rabelais*, first published in 1942 and made available in English as *The Problem of Unbelief in the Sixteenth Century* in 1982.[13] Here, Febvre shows his suitably stubborn preoccupation with the importance of historical context, especially when it comes to understanding the sensory histories of those under study. Febvre certainly valued historical imagination but not in the same way, or to the same extent, that Huizinga embraced it. Febvre was fascinated by the collection of facts not as an end in themselves but as a way to think about how someone in the sixteenth century would sense the world. He worked hard, according to one observer, not to rely on "his own twentieth-century eyes and ears." Febvre did not bequeath us a methodology as such but "something more like a code of conduct"—what I have elsewhere described as a "habit" of writing about history—that seems ideally suited to studying the senses, a way of remaining alert to sensory evidence whatever the particular historical source under consideration.[14]

Perhaps more than any other historian preceding him, Febvre took the senses seriously. In fact, he seems to have thought that in order to demonstrate his central thesis about the nature of religious belief in the sixteenth century, he was obliged to think carefully about the sensate. Whereas Huizinga used language to gesture broadly to the sensory atmospherics of an era, Febvre examined the senses because he believed they helped explain just how distant and different the mental world of the sixteenth century was. In chapter 12, "A Possible Support of Irreligion: Occultism," Febvre devotes roughly thirty pages to the sensory, with particular emphasis on "smells, tastes, and sounds."[15]

Febvre started from the premise that "we are hothouse plants; those men grew out of doors." "They were men close to the earth and to rural life, who encountered the countryside even in their cities, its plants and animals, its smells and noises." "They were," he wrote, "open-air men, seeing nature but also feeling, sniffing, hearing, touching, breathing her through all their senses." How did Febvre know this? Or, rather, why did he believe it? Because poets told him so. This is not the place to offer a formal critique of Febvre's reliance on sources. There is, in fact, quite a lot wrong with his reading. Not unlike Huizinga's treatment, Febvre's assumes a uniformity of sensory experience among all classes and genders, for example (for surely nobility did not experience touch in the same way as did peasants), and it also wrongly casts the present as somehow less sensate than the past when, in fact, we know this is far from the case. And, given the lyrical qualities of poetry, it is likely that the sensory evidence he culled from sixteenth-century poetry was inclined to support his larger case. In any event, Febvre read poetry in an effort to reveal something of the sensory world. Let us be clear: he is no Huizinga. He does not deploy his language to evoke a sensory past; instead, he offers a fidelity to what people—albeit carefully selected people—said about their sensory worlds. He reads enough poetry to conclude that, generally, his sixteenth-century historical actors were far more attuned to their senses and understood the world in more nonvisual ways than later generations did. If poetry is an accurate proxy for sixteenth-century experience, then the world was "full of sounds and laden with fragrances." Febvre is simply too good of a historian to rest his entire claim on the evocative nature of poetry, though, and happily scours letters and correspondence to push his claim that "the sixteenth century did not see first: it heard and smelled, it sniffed the air and caught sounds. It was only later, as the seventeenth century was approaching, that it seriously and actively became engaged in geometry. . . . It was then that *vision* was unleashed." Here, Febvre anticipates, with much more specificity than Huizinga, something akin to the argument later advanced by Ong and McLuhan concerning the way that print and science reworked the ratio of the sensory world in vision's favor. For now, though, in the sixteenth century, seeing was not believing and was not the exclusive source of knowledge or the sole arbiter of truth.[16]

Whatever the shortcomings of Febvre's treatment of the senses, his brush was not so impossibly broad as Huizinga's (whose work does not seem to have informed Febvre's thinking on the senses, at least if his footnotes are taken as reliable indicators), and he remained highly sensitive to context. More than that, Febvre seemed perfectly happy to think in multisensory terms. With sight playing a diluted role, Febvre seemed not to have worried about ranking the senses and instead approached sound, smell, and touch as intimately related—as synesthesia—and not especially susceptible to disaggregation. He properly treated the past as a multisensory universe, something that sensory history is only just beginning to do. He realized that his was hardly the last word on the topic and pointedly offered that "a series of fascinating studies could be done on the sensory underpinnings of thought in different periods," thereby, in effect, gesturing to the future of sensory history.[17]

One of the most important—if often unacknowledged, especially in English-speaking circles—early treatments of the senses was offered by French historian Robert Mandrou (1921–1984), another *Annales* School practitioner. Mandrou offered some pointed, helpful, and at times pressingly insightful observations about the importance of the senses. In his *Introduction à la France moderne: Essai de psychologie historique, 1500–1640*, first published in 1961 (translated and published in 1976 in English as *Introduction to Modern France, 1500–1640: An Essay in Historical Psychology*), Mandrou devotes a chapter to "the mind: senses, sensations, emotions, passions." Heavily influenced by Febvre (Mandrou dedicated the book to him), he frames the senses in a very particular way, treating them from an avowedly psychological perspective and as part of the mental equipment Febvre was so intent on understanding. At some level, Mandrou's treatment of the sensory is an unapologetic attempt to resurrect and perhaps rescue from relative historiographical obscurity the keen observations Febvre offered about the importance of the sensate in his final chapter in *The Problem of Unbelief*—an effort, as it were, to disseminate these insights more widely and circulate them in scholarly and even popular circles. Naturally, Mandrou draws on sources similar—sometimes identical—to those favored by Febvre, poetry in particular, on the grounds that the poets "were endowed with a sensibility which was perhaps no keener than that of the average man, but which expressed itself more readily." They offer us, he says, a way to "capture the sensory tonality of the first century of modern times." These were, says Mandrou, "men of sound rather than of sight."[18]

Like Huizinga and Febvre, Mandrou tends to frame his understanding of past sensory experience in oppositional terms and evinces a fondness for positing an "us" versus "them" sensory world. Sixteenth-century France, he says, witnessed the "development and use of different sense organs," in ways decidedly different from "ours." Sensory hierarchies were fundamentally different, he claims; sight "stood in third position, a long way behind hearing and touch." A certain environmental determinism enters his analysis here. Yes, says Mandrou, "the sense organs were the same as our own" but probably "sharper and more practiced in those times of continual violence, when constant vigilance was necessary." For these people "lived close to nature, which they touched, listened to and drank from in close quarters."[19]

Still, whatever the clumsiness of his environmental imperatives (and whatever the likelihood that Mandrou's claims on this front are accurate), he is probably on to something important when he shifts to the cultural forces behind sensory animation. Chief among these larger forces was religion. The rise of print and reading was, in the 1500s, not yet enough to promote the eye over the ear, according to Mandrou. In secular terms, most information was still conveyed by mouth to ear; religious faith was even more urgently a matter of listening and hearing because of scriptural and theological insistence on the preeminence of hearing God's word.[20]

Beyond the claim that sight was a secondary sense and that hearing was stubbornly important, sixteenth- and seventeenth-century French poets and, by extension, Mandrou himself seemed uncertain where and how to rank the proximate senses of taste, touch, and smell. "The poets were constantly touching and feeling," maintains Mandrou, asserting that until the eighteenth century (and perhaps after), "touch remained one of the master senses," with its ability to verify and even counter the sort of superficial, surface information conveyed by sight. But poets—people of the sixteenth century generally—were also highly olfactory. Even the ostensibly tactile act of kissing was heavily scented: "Quand de la lèvre à demi close / Je sens ton haleine de rose" (When from half-closed lips / Rose-scented breath I smell). Yet none of these senses carried the rationality later associated with sight, maintains Mandrou. While windows, spectacles, better lighting, microscopes, and optical instruments of scientific progress functioned to empower the eye at the end of the sixteenth century, the other senses remained tightly indexed to emotion, regardless, it seems, of the elevation of vision in the sensory hierarchy. Hearing, smelling, touching, and tasting all elicited emotional responses and, in Mandrou's estimation, were closely related to the occult and to violence, fired by the imagination of people who lived in dread of the night. In this tethering of the proximate senses to emotions, Mandrou helps establish, ironically enough, one of the long-standing conceits of history writ large: that modernity eclipsed the nonvisual senses by rendering them unreliable, irrational, unable to contain or capture truth and, ergo, unsuited to serious study. In other words, Mandrou here makes an association that later sensory historians will tackle head on and devote a great deal of effort to dismantling or, at the least, heavily revising.[21]

Whatever the shortcomings of *Modern France*, Mandrou teaches us something important about historical research on the senses. One of those lessons seems unwitting. For example, Mandrou is aware that his fondness for poetry is narrow and risks torquing evidence. He defends the decision on the basis that "the memorialists" have "little to offer by way of the immediate recording of sensations," a point that may well say something about the extent of sensory engagement more than it does about the inadequacy of the sources. What Mandrou might be pointing to here is the absence of (or heavily muted) sensory evidence that, in turn, tells us something about the sensory paucity of an age, an observation in direct contradistinction to his own argument, or it might simply be that diarists and letter writers rarely commented on the senses precisely because they were habituated and inured to them. While Mandrou does not ponder these matters, they serve as a powerful reminder to historians currently working on the history of the senses that sources matter and that silences might be as consequential as utterances.

The relative absence of commentary on certain sensory experiences at particular times might well indicate the declension of that sense or, indeed, its triumph.[22]

Mandrou is also helpful when it comes to reminding historians of the senses—especially those interested in historical acoustemology—of the importance of incorporating (or rather, reincorporating) music into our analyses. Mandrou maintains, quite rightly in my estimation, that music must be understood as part and parcel of a society's soundscape, a constitutive part of what people heard. It stood with noise and thunder and voice to function in myriad ways, religious and secular, and the exclusion of music from the sense of hearing—as has been the tendency in some recent writing on the history of sound—tends to desiccate the full texture of the auditory past.[23]

Notwithstanding Alain Corbin's sensible criticisms levelled against Guy Thuillier's book *Pour une histoire du quotidien au XIX* *siècle en Nivernais* (1977), it must be said that Thuillier, like Febvre and Mandrou, did important work in establishing the senses as a legitimate and helpful category of historical inquiry.[24] Thuillier offers his insights on the senses in a chapter on noises and sounds in a book otherwise dedicated to the quotidian aspects of life in the Nivernais in the nineteenth century. Fairly typical as a work of micro social history—popular in much historical writing at the time—the chapter on sound is nevertheless a careful and exceptionally innovative meditation on how to write a history of sound and listening. Thuillier is, preeminently, keenly aware of the difficulties and potential challenges of writing a history of "les bruits" and frames his discussion in that light. He makes several preliminary observations that would resonate with any scholar today working on historical acoustemology. He makes the point not only that noises "have a life and a death" but that we can, using written evidence, "date their appearance, their disappearance" and analyze how the sounds and noises are represented both in situ and in the context of memory. Silence, too, is important to Thuillier, "an essential element of every-day life," itself a topic that is only just beginning to earn the attention it deserves from, among others, Corbin himself.[25] The challenge is not inconsequential, says Thuillier. To capture the soundscape of a place and time is, he writes, something of an "impressionist" story, one guided by "small touches . . . and in-depth investigations" merely to identify the sounds of the past. While Thuillier indeed emphasizes the need to discover and document noises and sounds, he also, quite correctly, recognizes the central importance of deciphering their meaning. He does so in two ways. First, he points to the importance of the historic-ity of sounds: the meanings certain sounds and silences held for contemporaries and some of the systems those sounds served to underwrite (for example, how silence was used to establish disci-pline in schools and workshops and how people understood the absence of those sounds at the time). "The history of noises," he writes, "touches sociology, the history of daily life, and col-lective psychology." "What matters," he insists, "is the one who perceives, his expectations, his reactions," what Thuillier calls the "social fact" of sound, one emphasizing historically condi-tioned habits of listening. Second, he understands how our rec-ollection of the sounds of the past is put to work in the service of modern conceits about the past. "The old-fashioned noises of the past have become symbols of the peasant," says Thuillier. "The discreet hum of the spinning wheel, the cricket's song, the ticking of the clock": all, he suggests, perform the work of nos-talgia and powerfully—if inaccurately—inform our understand-ing of and beliefs about a particular group and place and time. Here, Thuillier shows himself to be a careful scholar of habits of listening as well as a narrator of sounds, and I think it fair to say that he anticipated by some forty years a few of the inter-pretive potholes that continue to beguile some historians of the senses generally. In roughly six pages of text (and nine pages of notes), not only does Thuillier manage to anticipate some much later key developments in writing on the history of sound, but he does so with an attentiveness to epistemological questions that serves us well today.[26]

If there is an overly mechanical quality to Thuillier's treatment, it is perhaps most evident in his tendency to index auditory shifts in perception to technological changes, which lends a certain whiggish, teleological quality to his analysis. Yet even here, Thuillier is careful not to posit clumsy breaks with the past. Technology did produce new noises, to be sure, but in dynamic, braided fashion: "to the traditional noise of hammers was added the . . . noise of the steam engines," he writes. He is also attentive to how new noises—such as the train, the automobile, industrial hammers—at first startle but, over time, become accepted key-notes, incorporated into the auditory world of listeners. Here, Thuillier anticipates the work of some scholars of technology and science who, in recent years, have done much to advance our understanding of listening habits in the context of technological change.[27]

Historians of the United States, while pioneering aspects of social history, were relatively slow to study the senses in any sustained fashion. While glimpses of interest in the sensate can be found in any number of US history books before the 1990s, few scholars offered any sustained contemplation about what the senses meant and how the historian could and should attend to them. Besides a pioneering article on the history of noise by Raymond Smilor, very few US historians actively pondered how, why, and whether the senses should be incorporated into their work.[28] Oscar Handlin (1915–2011) was an exception. It was in his most conservative work toward the end of his career, *Truth in History* (1979), that Handlin, the influential historian of immigration, attended to the sensory in sustained fashion. In this book, which at times amounted to a defense of traditional historical research against what he perceived as the fads of new scholarship and the concomitant partisanship he believed to be threatening the historical profession, Handlin devoted one of his seventeen chapters to the issue of "seeing and hearing" in the writing and researching of history.[29]

For Handlin, seeing and listening were important ways to access the past. How a historian saw the past was always an imperfect exercise to Handlin, because the nature of historical evidence is inherently murky. He gave the example of how difficult it was to see the past through, say, the eyes of a traveler whose sight was necessarily attuned to the new and not to the mundane or typical. He also believed it difficult to really see the past, "to look at rather than to read about" how an object, a town, a piece of art could be understood visually. As Handlin put it, "the indirect means of seeing must serve when the original has disappeared or is unavailable for direct inspection. But they do not substitute for the impression the knowledgeable historian gains from the original." Listening to the sounds of the past was also challenging, perhaps more so because "sound is not stone, and vanishes with the wind. The historian cannot catch the voices which echoed in the past."[30]

While Handlin seems sympathetic to Huizinga's call for a largely unmediated historical appreciation of the senses, he also warns that attempts to re-create the past using massive data sets—he mentions Colonial Williamsburg in this regard—court the danger of anachronism. A steady attention to context, in Handlin's opinion, is the antidote. When it came to visual evidence, Handlin counseled, "each culture and each period has its own way of treating perspective, space, line, and color, reflecting its own outlook."[31]

How best to put all of this into practice? Handlin stressed the importance of context. Yes, said Handlin, the historian can—and needs—to rely on the written descriptions of, say, a city, passed down by travelers and residents. But the limitations of these sources "cry out for reference to the surviving visual data": woodcuts, paintings, photographs, and the like. But even then, the historian "will not thereby have arrived at an understanding of what the city appeared to be to its earlier viewers. Only the borrowed eyes of the artists at the time can bring him that." Handlin seems to call for a sort of sensory immersion—looking, for example, through the eye of the artist—in a fashion that is context-specific but also bears a hint of (early) Huizinga's sensitivism. We are offered no concrete counsel on how to "borrow" the artist's eye beyond trying to think in the aesthetics and the mechanics of the era that produced the art.[32]

Handlin's thinking becomes a little clearer on the subject of hearing, although he thinks the topic more difficult than seeing because "sight may endure; the sound vanishes with the uttering." Attempts to reconstruct sounds, imagine how they were heard, and recover the meanings people attributed to them, says Handlin, can only partially succeed. Because sound and the ways in which it is heard depend on the auditory habits of the audience (their ways of listening), the environment and architecture, and even the weather, mood re-creation is something of a fool's errand and calls into question the very idea of historical re-creation as a desirable and achievable aim, even when the historian is armed with actual recordings of voice and song. For Handlin, then, context was essential for divining how sounds—and sights—were produced and experienced, with the proviso that such an understanding would always be imperfect because of the muted and limiting nature of historical evidence.[33] Handlin's counsel is helpful not least because it reminds us that the utmost care must be taken in using sensory evidence and that we should fear flirting with the seductive nature of that evidence.

## Foundations

The 1980s and 1990s were a critical period for sensory history. In these two decades, the history of the senses became something much more sustained, focused, and commented upon in the historical profession at large. The occasional forays into sensory history apparent before the 1980s were replaced by a growing body of work that not only attended to individual senses but increasingly examined multiple senses and witnessed calls for intersensory historical writing. This period was foundational insofar as it fertilized the field by framing sensory epistemologies and ontologies and establishing an intellectual trellis that still shapes the habit of sensory history to this day.

A broad and even inchoate collection of scholars performed this hard labor. They did so at a time when few historians took the senses seriously as a worthwhile or even doable historical project. For those who were not familiar with the early efforts of the *Annales* School to write the sensate into historical analysis, sensory history seemed something of a fool's errand. Surely the senses were biologically and psychologically determined and thus transcendent? Could the senses even have a history? Such a question was not uncommon. The work done in the 1980s and 1990s did a tremendous amount to change the conversation, shifting the terms from "Is there a history of the senses?" to "How and why did the senses change over time?" Many of the scholars publishing in this period were working in relative isolation from one another and drew on their own disciplinary specialties—which were often not rooted exclusively in historical work—to offer some remarkably thoughtful, often unique, and enduringly important works on the sensate. At base, the work published in the 1980s and 1990s tends to fall into one of three categories. It was a product of a given scholar's interdisciplinary background (which came from a variety of quarters); it was a reflection of a scholar's interest in making history more "relevant"; or, simply, it was written by Alain Corbin.

One of the enduring—and continuing—hallmarks of sensory history has been its avowed and unapologetic commitment to interdisciplinarity. In no small part, this was due to the kinds of writing offered in the 1980s and 1990s. Take, for example, Sander Gilman's 1988 study on hapticity, the immensely thoughtful *Goethe's Touch: Touching, Seeing, and Sexuality*. Gilman's scholarly background in German-language scholarship and Jewish studies was informed by his commitment to interdisciplinarity. These interests combined with his fascination with literary studies, cultural history, histories of the body, and the history of medicine (which, as a field, stood at the vanguard of developing a history of the senses in the 1990s, especially courtesy of the important work of Roy Porter) to give him the intellectual breadth and skill to write *Goethe's Touch* (which was published as an Andrew W. Mellon lecture in 1988 by the Graduate School of Tulane University). Up until then, very little had been written, at least explicitly, about the history of skin and tactility. And, despite the book's brevity, Gilman offered some foundational insights not just about the history of touch and touching but about the very epistemology underwriting its historical investigation. Gilman recognized that touch works both visually and more proximately and that a history of touch must remain keenly aware of historically situated conventions and habits governing touching, how it is viewed (quite literally), and how haptic protocols change over time. Touch, he quite properly maintained, is a social construction, and that essential fact requires us to understand the conventions surrounding the construction and the milieu in which they are born and iterated. Subsequent histories of touching and skin have taken that insight as fundamental.[34]

A similarly interdisciplinary path to sensory history—in this instance, the history of sound and listening—was charted by Paul Carter. In his 1992 work, *The Sound in Between: Voice, Space, Performance*, Carter, who ranks amongst the sharpest chroniclers and interpreters of colonialism, offered a wholly pathbreaking interpretation of the ways in which sound and auditory habits informed imperial encounters in Australia. Carter—a historian with extraordinarily broad interdisciplinary credentials—explored the contested history of a sound ("cooee") in a dazzling documentation of how the auditory world shaped colonialism, bound together white settlers, alienated Aboriginal peoples, and framed national identities. Again, though, the emphasis was on the context of discourse, the meaning of sounds uttered and heard in the time and place that they were generated and experienced.[35]

Avowed interdisciplinarity was (and remains) a key feature for other scholars pioneering the study of the senses. Few historians in the 1990s (and, indeed, after) have done as much to establish the importance of the senses historically as Constance Classen; no nonhistorian has done as much to popularize sensory history as anthropologist David Howes. Classen is a historian of religion with a keen understanding of ethnography and sensory anthropology. Her work, which began in the early 1990s and continues today, called for a heavily contextualized historical treatment of the sensate. Classen also was among the first historians of the senses to think transnationally, doing so from something of an *Annaliste* perspective that paid careful attention to change over time and profiling the essential importance of how context shaped the production and the meaning of the senses. Classen explored the sensory history of the Incas, focused on how the senses in a variety of places and times were culturally and historically constructed, highlighted the important role gender played in sensory formations, and was an essential voice in establishing the historical study of olfaction especially. Classen proved very adept, too, at tackling multiple senses and brought to bear her deep understanding of religion in an effort to unpack the historically specific meanings of the spiritual sensorium.[36] Like Classen—with whom he has worked closely—Howes helped establish the historical study of the senses beginning in the 1990s by theorizing and explicating sensory anthropology. Howes framed his work, at least in part, around the idea that the senses are culturally and historically constructed. It was this keen insight, as well as his pioneering call for a sustained examination of intersensoriality, that allows his work to speak so resonantly to historians.[37]

To say that the French historian Alain Corbin (1936–) has done more to establish and advance the study of sensory history than any other historian is not hyperbolic. In the 1980s and 1990s, Corbin pretty much popularized the field of sensory history by at once acknowledging the earlier *Annaliste* contributions to the study of the senses, by actively and thoughtfully critiquing their work, and by writing a series of foundational sensory histories.

Corbin is (refreshingly!) a difficult historian to categorize in part because he is immensely productive, having published almost a dozen books, many of which have been translated. While he writes in the tradition of the *Annales* School, he remains something of a maverick within that tradition. He often seems much more interested in the excavation of *mentalités* than he is in the sorts of social history that inform studies of the *longue durée* and collective structures, and he happily marries literary analysis with deeply empirical historical research.[38]

Here, I'll focus on Corbin's three main books that deal explicitly with the senses, all of which were either published or translated in the 1980s and 1990s. They are: *Le miasme et la jonquille: L'odorat et l'imaginaire social (XVIIIᵉ–XIXᵉ siècles)*, first published in French in 1982, then in English four years later as *The Foul and the Fragrant: Odor and the French Social Imagination*; *Le temps, le désir, et l'horreur,* published in 1991 and translated into English four years later as *Time, Desire, and Horror: Toward a History of the Senses*; and *Les cloches de la terre: Paysage sonore et culture sensible dans les campagnes au XIXᵉ siècle*, first published in Paris in 1994 and translated into English in 1998 as *Village Bells: The Culture of the Senses in the Nineteenth-Century French Countryside*.[39]

In *The Foul and the Fragrant*, Corbin pivots from Febvre not to deny the importance of smell in revealing the sensibility of an era but to challenge him on the timing of a shift. Febvre suggested, as we have seen, that it was in the sixteenth century that the sense of smell became diluted. Drawing on an extraordinary range of sources—manuals on medicine and hygiene, documents detailing urban history and architecture, histories of public health and science—and taking the sensory poetics of literature seriously, Corbin contended that Febvre had his timing wrong. It was not in the sixteenth century that France underwent a revolution in the olfactory social imagination; rather, it was between 1750 and 1850 that the sense of smell increased in its ability and power to locate, fix, discern, and discriminate. This century witnessed a pairing of scent and sensibility, lowering a culturally situated threshold of what constituted stench and inviting broad efforts at deodorization. Smell, he shows, was considered the basest of the senses in the eighteenth century, standing in stark contrast to the more truth-promoting eye. If the eighteenth century tolerated these baser animal scents, the nineteenth century did not. Rank bodily odors were replaced by "natural," often floral scents, and because these preferred scents were championed by elites, olfactory signatures and habits—what one smelled like, how one smelled—became a firm marker of class. In this way, Corbin not only wrote the history of smell into the history of urbanization in France; he actively claimed that olfaction was in and of itself an accurate proxy for modernization. Olfactory habits and thresholds, the ways in which smells and smelling were used to mark and frame social relations and cultural aesthetics, were highly dependent on context, Corbin shows, and by attending to those contexts he reliably identifies a hitherto occluded way of understanding the very process of modernization.

Corbin's *Time, Desire, and Horror: Toward a History of the Senses* is a unique book. Chief among its qualities is an effort to explicitly theorize the writing of the history of the senses, which he details in the chapter titled "A History and Anthropology of the Senses," itself arguably one of the earliest sustained meditations on the methodology of sensory history. Clues to Corbin's larger thinking are also apparent in the book's title: *Time, Desire, and Horror*. The senses, he suggests, are intimately linked to emotions: horror, desire, any number of emotions were indexed to sensory experiences and hitched to a specific context. "There is no other way," writes Corbin elsewhere, "to know men of the past than by trying to borrow their glasses and to live their emotions."[40]

One way to access Corbin's thinking is to examine his critique of Guy Thuillier's work. Despite—and because of—his reservations about it, Corbin helped place Thuillier's scholarship into the conversation about how to go about writing and researching sensory history. Corbin expressed some grave reservations about Thuillier's historical understanding of the senses, at least as outlined in Thuillier's *Pour une histoire du quotidien*.[41] For Corbin, Thuillier approached the history of the senses from a positivist perspective and tried to trace the contours and evolution of the sensory environment by drawing up "an inventory of the sensations which were present at a given moment in history in each social milieu." Thuillier, argued Corbin, essentially "attempted to compile a catalogue and measure the relative intensity of the noises which might reach the ear of a villager in the Nivernais in the middle of the nineteenth century." This approach was "by no means negligible." In Corbin's estimation, "it aids immersion in the village of the past; it encourages the adoption of a comprehensive viewpoint; it helps to reduce the risk of anachronism." Indeed, says Corbin, reading Thuillier, "you can almost hear, as you read this book, the ringing of the hammer on anvil, the heavy thud of the wooden mallet wielded by the cartwright, the insistent presence of bells and the whinny of horses in an aural environment where the noise of the engine or the amplifier was unknown." All seductive stuff, even for Corbin. But not quite seductive enough. Corbin's critique is worth quoting in full. Thuillier's treatment of the senses, he says—in this instance, hearing— "is based on a questionable postulate, it implies the non-historicity of the modalities of attention, thresholds of perception, significances of noises, and configuration of the tolerable and the intolerable. In the last analysis, it ends up by denying the historicity of that balance of the senses. . . . It is as if, in the eyes of the author, the habitus of the Nivernais villager of the nineteenth century did not condition his hearing, and so his listening."[42] Corbin is doing something fundamentally important here, something that, as I will later argue, is relevant to the future of sensory-historical writing: he is actively engaging and critiquing the work of a colleague and, moreover, doing so by stressing the importance of contextualization to the enterprise of sensory history. While Corbin's criticisms are wholly compelling and legitimate, as Corbin himself says, "Guy Thuillier's project deserves, nevertheless, to be refined." A good deal of what historians of the senses have been up to in the last couple of decades is, in essence, a project of refinement, even if Thuillier's work is very rarely acknowledged as an important basis for it.[43]

Seemingly in an effort to refine Thuillier's project, Corbin's *Village Bells: The Culture of the Senses in the Nineteenth-Century French Countryside* is an exercise in how to listen historically. At base, this remarkable book asks readers to listen not with their ears but with the ears of the nineteenth-century French. Corbin is especially interested, as he was with olfaction, in tracing shifts in sensory thresholds and contextualizing the meaning of auditory landscapes. Central to this exercise in "listening to listening" were the remarkable number of disputes in the French nineteenth-century countryside over the meaning of bells. The French Revolution led to the removal and destruction of many bells from rural communities, principally as a way for secular forces to undermine the religious authority associated with bell ringing. There is irony here: the removal of bells did nothing to diminish local communities' desire for them, and they reacquired them whenever possible. What did change, though, was the use to which bells were put. Certainly, they retained their religious function, calling people to mass, for example. Secular sounds joined religious ones in the nineteenth century so that the bells now also signaled the times of markets, oriented travelers, sounded political events, and coordinated daily social life. Not that these matters were uncontested, especially in the period from 1830 to 1870. Those who controlled the timing of the bell ringing exercised cultural and political authority over their villages. In a good example showing how meaning was not always indexed to the volume or size of bells, Corbin reveals how, even as bells became larger and louder, their meaning changed, especially during the 1860s–80s. New technologies intervened that served to limit the cultural purchase of bell sounds and their ability to define the auditory landscape. Private clocks and calendars, for example, both quieter than the village bells, became important. New sounds competed: electric motors and steam engines populated the soundscape with sounds not only louder and new but different in meaning and authority. Corbin listens to listeners and charts shifts in the ways that sounds either lost or gained meaning. He details the delicate interplay between actual ways of listening and actual changes in the physical environment. Corbin bequeathed a great deal to writing on the history of the senses, but perhaps his most important (and continuing) legacy was his insistence on the need to properly situate and contextualize the senses of the past so that their meaning was understood through the noses, eyes, ears, skins, and tongues of the participants.

Besides Handlin, relatively few historians of the United States delved into the sensory past before the mid-1990s. Not only was George H. Roeder Jr. an exception, but his important—if often overlooked—1994 article explains why. Roeder's essay was essentially a survey of how and why (or why not) US history textbooks deployed sensory references. Roeder's blunt conclusion was simple: his analysis of sixteen commonly used US history textbooks revealed that "ours is a nearly sense-less profession." Part of Roeder's argument was based on his experience teaching in history departments (where the extent of sensory evidence was summed up in "the clangor of nearby construction, glaring sunlight, flatulent students") and his time teaching in an art school (where "going to work means encountering the smell of linseed oil, the acrid taste of the fumes produced by etching fluids, . . . and the sounds of . . . kinetic sculpture.") More substantively, Roeder examined sixteen textbooks published in the past forty years for "analytically significant smells, tastes, sights, sounds, and tactile sensations." His main findings were threefold. First, when textbooks did invoke the senses, they did so overwhelmingly in the negative: "experiences presented as disgusting, oppressive, painful, or meretricious carried almost the entire burden of instructing students that the people they were reading about were sentient creatures, influenced by the sensorial environment." Second, textbooks published after 1970 tended to take the senses more seriously by incorporating sensory descriptions into the narrative. Still, the vast majority of sensory descriptions were still negative: if smells appeared, they were bad. The overall inattention to the senses was, believed Roeder, damaging to students: "When they leave school without the conceptual or linguistic skills to understand or even identify the sensory features of the society they live in or of those they encounter in their studies and travels, historians bear part of the responsibility."[44]

Why the shift after 1970? Roeder suggests several factors, including the greater willingness by social and cultural historians to embrace the sensate and developments in the larger culture, such as attitudes toward sexuality. Roeder was careful to point out that sensory histories required no new or innovative techniques—sensory meaning could be culled from the written word.

Roeder was also careful to make the case—one that, I think, has shaped quite a lot of later thinking—that sensory history offers a viable and enduring way to write a kind of history more accessible to the general public, a way for historians to engage a popular audience. This last point was important for the future writing of sensory history, especially after 2000. It not only helped give rise to a sustained (and noble) effort to use the senses to broaden the appeal of written and "lived" history but also unwittingly invited, and even encouraged, a partial retreat from the very historicism and contextualization that Corbin and others were arguing was essential to the evolution of the field.[45]

# CHAPTER 2

# Present

## Beyond Booming

Nearly two decades ago, in 2000, Douglas Kahn described the growth of sound studies—especially the history of sound—as booming.[1] If he was right then about historical acoustemology, now the study of the history of sound, especially, and sensory history more generally can be reliably characterized as deafening. To be sure, the study of the different senses has proceeded unevenly since Kahn made his claim, and it continues to suffer from an asymmetry. There is far more work on sound and historical acoustemology than, say, on the history of smell, taste, and touch, and in this respect, historical writing on the senses mirrors the putative sensory hierarchy we have inherited from the Enlightenment. I think, then, it is probably true that the field of sound studies, for example, has "crystalised, if not ultimately 'emerged,'" while the other senses, with the exception of vision, have been less studied.[2] Still, we do have an unprecedented number of articles, collected essays, and books on any number of aspects of sensory history. Various subdisciplines and virtually all areas and periods of historical study seem positively enchanted with sensing the past. We have, for example, deeply impressive work on the subject from scholars of science and technology, American studies, and historians of all periods of American history, not to mention historians of the ancient world, Australia, and modern Europe. And while we are in dire need of much more work on the senses in Asian history, the little that has been done is exemplary. On the whole, we are now cataloging every conceivable sound, noise, and silence, smell, taste, and touch, and sight and ways of seeing from an incredible range of periods and places.[3]

Building on the foundational work of the 1990s, the period between 2000 to the present (an arbitrary designation, I know, but one useful for assessing the scale and rate of sensory history production and interest) saw a marked uptick in sensory history publications in a variety of forms. While the majority of these were, and are, dedicated to the history of sound and listening, many were, and are, not. There is no one metric, of course, but some developments point emphatically to the fact that not only is sensory history now established, but it promises to grow even more. For example, forums on aspects of the history of the senses, published in preeminent journals, highlight the interest in the subject. A few examples will suffice. In 2008, the *Journal of American History* hosted a roundtable called "The Senses in American History." Three years later, in 2011, the *American Quarterly* published "Sound Clash: Listening to American Studies," and the *American Historical Review* published a forum on "The Senses in History." The premier journal for public history, *The Public Historian*, hosted a roundtable exchange on sound, listening, and noise in 2015; the *Radical History Review*, also in 2015, devoted a volume to critical listening to the past; and the *Hispanic American Historical Review* dedicated a forum to historical acoustemology a year later, in 2016.[4]

Book series dedicated to sensory history also point to the importance of the field, involving as they do significant financial investment on the part of presses and the availability of dedicated editors. Since 2014, for example, Routledge has published seven important books in its series The Senses in Antiquity, under the impressive editorship of Mark Bradley and Shane Butler.[5] For several years now, David Howes has edited two very important series at Bloomsbury, the Sensory Studies Series and the Sensory Formations Series, both of which, while multidisciplinary, hold enormous appeal and intellectual reward for historians of the senses.[6] My own series, Studies in Sensory History, published by the University of Illinois Press (2011–18), produced nine exceptional books; a new series published by Penn State University Press, Perspectives in Sensory History, for which I serve as series editor (and of which this book is a part), promises to further expand the appeal and reach of sensory history. Cambridge University Press's Elements Series, Histories of Emotions and the Senses, edited by Jan Plamper, offers some highly innovative volumes inviting scholars of sensory studies to think in terms of the history of emotion.[7] In related fashion, collaborators in the Cambridge Russian Sensory Network (CRUSH), which focuses on twentieth-century Russian sensory history, have produced an impressive array of articles and monographs and, in effect, have made the sensory turn in Russian and Slavic studies important and enduring.[8]

Not insignificantly, sensory studies has its own journal, *The Senses and Society*. Established in 2006, the journal is now in its fifteenth volume and is an increasingly influential platform for the interdisciplinary study of the senses, frequently publishing work by historians. There is also the immensely helpful and innovative Centre for Sensory Studies, hosted by Concordia University, which has done an enormous amount to encourage the study of the senses generally and sensory history specifically.[9]

Edited readers are also a helpful index to the state and growth of a field, designed as they often are to introduce a new generation of scholars—students in particular—to a new topic by way of reprinting foundational pieces. They have proliferated. Between 2000 and 2005, we saw the publication of Michael Bull and Les Back's *Auditory Culture Reader* (2003), Veit Erlmann's *Hearing Cultures* (2004), my own *Hearing History* (2004), and Carolyne Korsmeyer's indispensable *The Taste Culture Reader: Experiencing Food and Drink* (2005). The trend has only continued: *The Oxford Handbook of Sound Studies*, edited by Trevor Pinch and Karin Bijsterveld, was published in 2011; Jonathan Sterne produced *The Sound Studies Reader* a year later; and, most recently, Michael Bull edited *The Routledge Companion to Sound Studies* in 2018.

Multivolume treatments are also helpful indicators of the importance of a field, and sensory history has not come up short in this category. For example, Constance Classen's 2014 set of volumes on sensory history covers a long temporal arc and has considerable geographic reach. Although I will say more about this magnificent set later, consider the sheer temporal and geographic range of each of the six volumes, not just in terms of material covered but also in terms of the editors for each volume. Paying attention to these details gives us a good idea of just how established, ecumenical, and broad the field of sensory history is. For example, the first volume, *A Cultural History of the Senses in Antiquity, 500 BCE–500 CE,* is edited by Jerry Toner of the University of Cambridge; the second collects essays by historians covering the senses during the Middle Ages (500–1450) and is edited by Richard Newhauser of Arizona State University.

Herman Roodenburg, of the University of Amsterdam, presents a wide range of essays on the sensory Renaissance (1450–1650), for the third volume; and Anne Vila, of the University of Wisconsin–Madison, edits the fourth volume, *A Cultural History of the Senses in the Age of Enlightenment, 1650–1800*. Volumes 5 and 6 cover the Age of Empire (1800–1920), edited by Constance Classen of McGill University, and the senses in the Modern Age (1920–2000), edited by David Howes of Concordia University. These volumes offer a clear indication of just how international the study of sensory history has become.

Likewise, in 2018, Bloomsbury published David Howes's magnificent four-volume edited collection, *Senses and Sensation: Critical and Primary Sources*, volume 2 of which is dedicated to the history and sociology of the senses. With this collection, Howes has doubtlessly provided current and future students of the senses with an enduringly useful set of essential texts that will help the field of sensory studies generally, and specifically sensory history, flourish.

Perhaps the most reliable indicator of any field's growth is the number of published monographs. Monographs indicate not only the interest among practitioners but commitments from university and commercial presses. Consider just US history. Sensory history generally began to capture the interest of American historians in the late 1990s, with a number of monographs appearing in print in the early 2000s. Studies of sound, hearing, and listening led the way with at least four important monographs appearing in print in a three-year period, 2000–2003. Why US historians elected to write about sound before turning to the other senses remains unclear. It was probably a result of multiple factors, including the availability of much earlier and important theoretical work on soundscapes by R. Murray Schafer and an interest in engaging the "Great Divide" theory, which detailed the replacement of older senses, such as

intuition, with a new sensory hierarchy, headed by sight, and
the concomitant degradation of the proximate senses of smell,
sound, taste, and touch—a theory most famously associated
with media theorists Marshall McLuhan and Walter Ong. Add to
these the influence of European historiography, which attended
first to sound, hearing, and listening, itself partly influenced by
the established work by musicologists, and the particular interests of some subfields—such as the history of religion and medicine—which placed an emphasis on the importance of sound as
a way to further interrogate key developments in those fields.[10]
Regardless of the particular reasons behind individual scholars'
choices, we saw books published on the history of sound and
hearing during the Second Great Awakening (2000); the auditory history of slavery, free labor, and antebellum sectional-
ism (2001); a history of American architectural acoustics and
modernity in the early twentieth century (2002); and the history of sound and acoustemology in colonial America (2003).
Since then, other monographs have expanded our understanding of how sound (and silence) shaped several developments in
American history.[11]

## Dividends

Why should historians generally consider incorporating the
sensate into their analyses? Why have an increasing number of
historians elected to turn to the sensory in their particular subfields of historical expertise? What are the dividends of attending
to smell, sound, taste, and touch and bringing these senses into
conversation with conventional "eyewitness" testimony? What
do we learn through such endeavors, and what does the historical profession risk by not embracing the sensate? Let me try
to answer these questions first by highlighting some work that
speaks to historians of all periods and places, work that shows

that the senses were thoroughly veined into all sorts of social, political, economic, and cultural relations, events, and periods— and that to properly and fully understand developments in those times and places, we must include the sensate.

I think it is true to say that historians still rely most heavily on sight when discussing testimony of the past. We talk about historical "observers," prize the analytical "lens" of history, and are driven by, among other factors, the Enlightenment desire for "perspective." After all, we are heirs to processes and technologies that have privileged sight over the other senses. The invention of print trained us to read silently, with the eye becoming more important than the ear as a receiver of information. Think, too, of photographs, telescopes, spectacles. The idea that seeing is believing is embedded deeply in Western culture.

Sensory historians have been working to correct this overreliance by restoring the other senses of taste, touch, smell, and hearing to our understanding of the past. Some of the dividends of the sensory approach are on display in the aforementioned six-volume *A Cultural History of the Senses* from Bloomsbury, under the general editorship of historian Constance Classen. To recap: the collection is incredibly broad, with volumes covering Antiquity, the Middle Ages, the Renaissance, the Age of Enlightenment, the Age of Empire, and the Modern Age. As general editor, Classen innovatively and skillfully frames each volume around certain thematic domains. Each volume examines sensory culture in light of nine major domains and historical developments: social life, urban sensations, the marketplace, religion, philosophy and science, medicine, literature, art, and media. This domain-based approach not only allows for a fuller, more textured, and interpretively robust treatment of the senses across time and space but also invites us to consider how the senses operated in dialogue, how they interacted, in useful and revealing ways. By taking this ingenious approach, the collection allows us to think in new and productive ways about intersensoriality across time and space.[12]

What do we learn from this collection that a nonsensory or exclusively visualist approach denies us? These volumes, generally sensory histories, teach us great deal. More than quantitatively expanding our understanding of a place and time, the senses help us better understand how given people, times, and places were constituted sensorially. Antiquity, to take one example, was not a world in which the five senses had distinct registers. Instead, people muddled them, producing "synesthesia," a mixing up of the senses: Homer's famous descriptions of the "wine-dark sea" braided sight, taste, and smell. Literature also offered a different type of sensory experience. With perhaps less than 10 percent of people functionally literate, writers wrote to be heard and strove to evoke the sensate. As Silvia Montiglio puts it in her essay on the senses in ancient Greek literature, "Greek literature caresses not only the ears. Verbal persuasion could be felt to work through other senses as well, to have an impact on sight and even touch as well as hearing." Now, certainly, the later Roman world was also a highly visual one, where colors indicated social standing. White was the cheapest color, followed by red, then yellow; blue and black were reserved for great rooms in villas. But even here, nonvisual senses were critical for other reasons, with statue-touching and incense-burning essential for connecting with the divine.[13]

In the Middle Ages, the relationship between the sensory world and faith became especially pronounced, but advances in the physical sciences and medicine were also driven by sensory experimentation. Physicians felt pulses, smelled plague, and used taste to diagnose disease. Neither were the senses static or even wholly reliable. Renaissance sensory theory included the inner senses (the common sense, the imagination, and memory) in addition to the customary five senses; how they interacted was of great import, too. In this period, a sensory uncertainty prevailed, thanks to emerging urban environments and the growth of the marketplace. Mountebanks were everywhere and early moderns relied on all their senses to ascertain good from bad, true from false. Salt was tested by touch; ears verified the quality of glass; noses sniffed the legitimacy of perfumes.[14]

Even the putatively hypervisual age of the Enlightenment was awash with sensory experience. This age witnessed encounters with new people and new parts of the world, notably what some European settlers called the "howling wilderness" of early America and all the gustatory, auditory, visual, and tactile experiences associated with the New World. In this period, homes became physically more comfortable, warmer, and quieter. Foods, at least for elites and the emerging middle classes, were stimulating and new. Heavily spiced food, coffee, tea, tobacco, chocolate, and increasing amounts of sugar made their way into diets. So potent were these experiences that the period had a quality of sensory overload, inducing a sort of nervous sensibility from feeling too much. This was very much in keeping with what historian Peter Burke describes as a hyperstimulation of the senses in the urban environments of the Renaissance world.[15]

Modernity, too, was fully sensory. If we exclude the nonvisual senses from our histories of, for example, imperialism, industrialism, large-scale urbanization, and a host of other nineteenth- and twentieth-century developments, we are left with a partial and warped understanding of these fundamental processes. The modern era introduced new smells and ways of smelling, for example. Cities and bodies were increasingly deodorized, courtesy of sewer systems and soap, often at the behest of elites who feared—but also did much to advance—the association between fetor, disease, and the working classes. Automobiles, electricity, radio, television, and the widespread use of plastics all changed what people saw, heard, and felt.[16]

My point here is simple. What we know of the past, especially in the West, is not only expanded significantly by Classen's *A Cultural History of the Senses*; rather, our long, muddled, complicated history is, in many ways, constituted by the senses. Writing the sensate out of this history leaves us impoverished, partial, and (dare I say) blind.

In extended fashion, I conclude this chapter with three examples designed to illustrate the importance of attending to the sensate in historical writing. One is from the history of sound, showcasing how an attention to the heard world can inform scholarship in article format. The second is an example of how a contextualized sensory history can help us make better sense of our own historical moment, and the third example shows how attention to the history of touch can inform even the most traditional form of historical writing. All three examples make the point that a history without the senses is not only impoverished but also fails to grant us access to how structures and belief systems are made, how countries are formed, how groups are empowered and subjugated, how our understanding of our sensory present is often beholden to our reading of our sensory pasts, and how historical memory itself is shaped. In other words, not to sense the past deadens us to critically important developments, ones that will remain occluded and opaque if we ignore the habit of sensory history.

Key works on historical acoustemology have charted the history of how sounds, habits of listening, and silences were contested, were argued over, and drove forward historic moments. To some extent, this is to be expected: scholars of US historical acoustemology, especially, have written within preexisting historiographies, attending to debates within, for example, colonial America or modern US history.[17] I will offer just one example here, which, to my mind, demonstrates the dividends of aural history.

This example is Sarah Keyes's pioneering essay "'Like a Roaring Lion': The Overland Trail as a Sonic Conquest," published in the June 2009 issue of the *Journal of American History*. According to Keyes, the history of westward expansion in the nineteenth century by Euro-Americans (or Overlanders, as they were sometimes called, after the Overland Trail) into Native American territories cannot be properly or fully understood unless we pay attention to sound. Native peoples, she argues, understood westward expansion as "a sonic conquest." The Overlanders, by contrast, noted in their diaries and letters the possible "aural impact" on the American West and its inhabitants. They "portrayed their sounds," says Keyes, "as having the power to subdue the savage wilds and help transform the West into American territory." Keyes is interested mainly in explaining "how overlanders' self-described aural penetration helped advance American expansion." She shows how "the aural is inextricably intertwined with struggles for dominion and power." Overlanders "interpreted environmental sounds and silences to render unfamiliar territory recognizable, knowable, and therefore capable of being possessed," naming landmarks in Anglo-auditory terms ("Bellowing Rock," "Echo Canyon," "Steamboat Springs") and thereby incorporating western, "alien" land into an American domain and domesticating the putatively "foreign" through an appeal to their familiar auditory lexicon. But Keyes's larger point is that recovering the "sonic dimension of the Overland Trail restores a part of American history more often commemorated than analyzed to a central place in our understanding of the process of conquest." Keyes understands the violence of the westward treks as constituted by sounds, noises, and silences, and she stresses the transgressive nature of the auditory. Sounds punch their way into ears, even if those ears do not want to hear. And for this reason alone, if we are to understand fully the nature of US westward expansion, if we are to account for the full range of violence integral to the process, we must listen.[18]

My second example aims to show how what we have learned about the sensory past, at least in the West, enables us to make better sense of very recent history. Here, I ponder the sensory history of COVID-19 and the global pandemic of 2020 which, as of this writing, threatens to continue into the foreseeable future.[19]

The work of sensory historians allows us to place very recent events into appropriate historical perspective. Judging by this work, it seems increasingly apparent that, courtesy of COVID-19, humanity is undergoing a sensory revolution. All of the senses have been affected by the coronavirus pandemic—not because the senses themselves have changed but because the context and environment in which we sense has been profoundly altered.

For the most part, sensory historians find that sensory shifts and perceptions tend to happen very slowly, with changes in sensory habits measured in decades and centuries, not in weeks and months. After all, the very idea that there are only five distinct senses took ages to mature, gaining credence in the Enlightenment. This period not only discounted erstwhile senses (such as the sense of "intuition") but also arranged the five senses into a distinctive hierarchy. While sensory historians have rightly interrogated and challenged the extent to which sight really triumphed (and the extent to which the other senses were degraded), rhetorically, at least, many contemporaries believed that the Enlightenment and the Age of Reason and the science underwriting them empowered the eye as the sense of truth. Smell, taste, touch, and, to a lesser extent, hearing—senses that had once been held in high esteem in the ancient and medieval worlds—supposedly lost their currency and became less reliable as arbiters of truth and knowledge.[20]

The point I wish to stress here is that these changes, exaggerated though they are, took time. Seeing was, increasingly, believing by about 1800, but it had taken centuries for the original iteration of the phrase, "seeing is believing, but feeling's the truth," to lose its tactile quality.

The Western sensorium intact, the nineteenth century ushered in some profound and long-term changes in how people used and understood their senses. Olfaction offers a good example. Western noses became more refined, more sensitive, and more alert to noxious smells. Rank and fetid smells gave way to a world that valued pleasant and deodorized smells. Noses that could detect the difference were applauded. As Corbin showed, public health and aesthetics were at work here. Physicians advised that foul smells had to be shuttled underground and consigned to sewers, lest the stench itself cause disease. Even after the advent of germ theory in the 1890s, public health experts still associated stench with ill-health. Bodies, in turn, should be washed, even disinfected. This olfactory evolution in smells and habits of smelling took a couple of centuries.[21]

Now, think of the sensory changes that have taken place in just a matter of months as a result of the coronavirus and the policies put in place to contain it and mitigate its effects.

The most obvious point to make here is that the authority of the Enlightenment eye has been undermined. Eyes cannot locate this invisible enemy; seeing is no longer believing. But if the cause of COVID-19 is invisible, its effects are emphatically not. Desolate city streets are new sights; the absence of contrails strikes many as almost primordial; masks render once familiar faces unrecognizable.[22]

Within a matter of months, soundscapes have changed, as have habits of listening. Coronavirus spreaders are sometimes described as "silent." Auditory holes now litter the soundscape. Urban dwellers hear less traffic, the closure of many schools means that the sounds of children laughing and playing in public are rapidly becoming a distant memory, and the cancellation of many religious services has greatly reduced the sound of bells in some communities. Once smothered sounds—such as birdsong—now come to the auditory fore, especially in towns. The sound is not new, but the effects of COVID-19 have turned up the volume. In some ways, human voices are louder because there are no whispers at six feet.[23]

The sense of smell has been hit hard. To breathe, after all, is to smell. If you can. Anosmia—the loss of the sense of smell—is an early sign of infection. Even if we keep our sense of smell, people now often pause before they inhale lest they breathe in an enemy they cannot see.[24]

Taste is no longer as easily sated and palates are rearranged. Restaurants still cater, but in take-out fashion and with less variety. Hot food once served in-house is colder and less palatable after having been transported to the more distant dining-room table. Certain staples—milk, eggs, meat—are harder to find in certain locations.[25]

Touch is the obvious sensory casualty in all of this. Centuries of handshaking habits have evaporated; in the United States, high fives are gone. Public hugs, kisses, and nuzzles have all been lost with the fear of infection. One of the short-term—and, possibly, long-term—effects of coronavirus public policy has been what amounts to a domestication and even privatization of tactility. People touch in private now; tactility is limited to family members. Those living alone are undergoing a tactile revolution of their own. They rarely touch other human beings. Public touching, then, is scarce and even once common tactile habits, such as the touching of vegetables and fruits in grocery stores, seem diminished.[26]

Sensorially, there has been nothing like this. Even the violence done to the senses by wars, hurricanes, tornadoes, and earthquakes is modest in scale and scope compared to this sensory revolution. No war or natural disaster has impacted as many people so rapidly. The global sensory impact of the coronavirus is a product of technology and speed. The virus spread so quickly because of technology (most obviously, air travel); news of the virus was disseminated quickly and broadly courtesy of the Internet. The mechanisms for attempting to check the spread of the virus—and the sensory consequences of those policies—are rapid and thoroughly global. No pandemic has spread so far so rapidly in human history.

Possible legacies are hard to fathom. Beyond the deaths, there will likely be victims of word and culture. Sensory turns of phrases will change. The results will not be even. Thanks to virtual communication, "see ya" and "I hear ya" should remain stable, but "staying in touch" and "getting a grip" could go the way of the sensory dinosaur.

If normalcy eludes us, a whole new world of sensory engagement will emerge, and it could be terrifying. Our soundscape could be of civil strife, punctuated with the smell of tear gas and the resounding sting of rubber bullets on flesh.[27] If quarantine and social distancing remain the norm, perhaps the coronavirus will accelerate what has long been in the works: a post-human sensorium in which the senses, especially touch, detach from the human body and begin to inhabit a virtual environment whereby technology enables the virtual simulacrum of touch and, in the long run, assumes the reality of hapticity.[28] Whatever the changes, keeping in mind the sensory history we have excavated to date will help us understand the sensory history of the present and, possibly, the future.

My final, more extended, example illustrates in some detail how arguably the most traditional form of historical writing—biography—can benefit enormously from the application of the habit of sensory history and, in the process, help us make better sense of our own contemporary moment. Specifically, I want to show what paying attention to touch can tell us about Abraham Lincoln, arguably the United States' most famous president. Not only does attending to touch reliably convey something that contemporaries thought important (Lincoln's skin), but it does so by highlighting how text and material culture can grant us access to an understanding of how touch was—and, indeed, still is—mediated by context and the imperatives of a particular time and place.

To think of historical biographies in terms of the senses goes against a deeply ingrained conceit. Implicit in a good deal of historical biography is a way of understanding the past that privileges the eye. That is, it is written not only about men and women from their point of view but also from the perspective of their—and their contemporaries'—eyes. Almost all biographical work inquires from the vantage point of how the subject "saw" the world or how the world envisioned them; precious few ask how their subjects sensed the world and how the world perceived them in nonvisual terms.[29] Think of what follows, then, as an invitation to see how a sensory history can work with even the most tenaciously visual genre of historical writing.

Abraham Lincoln was and remains one of America's most iconographic presidents, which is to say that we see him, visualize him, picture him, and process him through the eye. And with good reason. He was the first President photographed at his inauguration and his image was disseminated very widely. His image lingers in and on things: on US pennies and five-dollar bills, in marble and granite, on statues, and in photographs.[30]

But there was more to Lincoln than meets the eye. There was also his skin. Taking Lincoln's skin seriously—thinking about how what David Howes has called the "dermalogical turn" can be applied to historical biography, reading images (and texts) depicting Lincoln's tactility, his skin, his hapticity—can prick our appreciation of how he understood touch and how his touch was perceived by contemporaries. This, in turn, can tell us a great deal about Lincoln himself, the nature of antebellum democracy, the origins and elaboration of Lincoln's and antebellum America's emotional landscape (notably an emerging humanitarian, antislavery sentiment), the historical construction of Lincoln's memory in popular culture, and the history of touching and not touching physical representations of Lincoln, specifically, and public monuments generally.[31]

Lincoln's skin was important to contemporaries. It was perceived as rough, flinty, and leathery, a product of outside labor, accentuated by the wart on his right cheek and scar over his right eye. The wiry beard grown in 1861 and his scarred hands only added to the perception. Moreover, Marfan syndrome may have played a role in texturing Lincoln's skin. The syndrome, while most obviously manifested in significant height and enlarged hands and feet, also affects the skin. Many people with Marfan syndrome develop stretch marks, lending the skin a leathery look. While we do not know with any certainty that Lincoln had the Marfan gene, experts think it likely that he had a mild variation of the condition.[32]

Contemporary interest in Lincoln's skin was in keeping with an antebellum political culture that valued hapticity. Handshaking was the *sine qua non* of political touch and had something of a democratic ring to it, a rough equality associated with the nineteenth-century idea of "true honor" and notions of white masculinity. Elected and electable leaders had to touch voters, directly and indirectly, physically and emotionally.[33]

Lincoln was a prodigious handshaker. It helped give rise to his reputation as a strong, egalitarian, common man, one in touch with the people. For example, he had a marathon and physically arduous handshaking session in New York in February 1861 as president-elect. Just after his election as president, according to one contemporary, Lincoln met with crowds whose "hand-shaking . . . was something fearful," with "every man in the crowd . . . anxious to wrench the hand of Abraham Lincoln. He finally gave both hands to the work, with great good nature." On his way from Springfield, Illinois, to Washington, DC, in 1861, Lincoln stood at the end of a railway car, glad-handing voters. And just before his assassination, Lincoln shook hands "with over six thousand soldiers" at City Point Hospital.[34]

Literally, Lincoln's hands and skin recorded politics. According to the Massachusetts senator Charles Sumner, even Lincoln's signature on the 1863 Emancipation Proclamation was riddled with the common touch because "he had been shaking hands all the morning, so that his writing was unsteady." Lincoln commented, "When people see that shaky signature they will say 'See how uncertain he was.' But I was never surer of anything in my life." The signature was in his hand and of his hand, shot through with the touch of politics. The only cast of Lincoln's hands, taken by Leonard W. Volk in Springfield, Illinois, on the Sunday after Lincoln's nomination in 1860, is deeply inscribed with a history of handshaking. Volk took the cast after "thousands" had gone to Lincoln's home, "passing through the house in single file, each citizen giving Lincoln a vigorous handshake." The cast tells the story of touch: "The swollen muscles that resulted from this reception are quite noticeable in the cast," according to its owner, essayist Laurence Hutton.[35]

Handshaking as practiced by Lincoln helped disassociate the old connection between touch and disease and elevate touch to a rational, learned position. Understanding the political consequences of touch under burgeoning American democracy helps temper extravagant claims concerning the premodern, irrational quality of hapticity, especially those made by Immanuel Kant. For Kant, the physical, direct nature of touch rendered it an unexamined form of knowledge. Conversely, Kant considered sight thoroughly detached, distanced, and reflective, less emotional and more rational. The history of political handshaking in antebellum America suggests otherwise. The thrill of touching Lincoln's hand was at once immediate and emotional, connecting the common man to the president himself; it was also touch in the service of modern democracy, a haptic language that shaped image and political authority and was understood as revealing the truth about a person's character.[36]

Skin color rather than skin texture has haunted historical imagination to the point that few scholars of antebellum America conceive of skin as having anything but a visual quality.[37] To appreciate Lincoln's understanding of slavery fully, we need to investigate his appreciation of skin and the more general relationship between hapticity and ideas about interiority, feeling, emotion, and humanitarianism.

Lincoln's understanding of touch, skin, slavery, and humanitarianism was intimately tied to what Norbert Elias identified as the "civilizing process," a broadly constituted process that wrought some important changes on ideas concerning the meaning, function, and form of touch. The disciplining of the self that Elias described as an essential component of modernity interiorized aspects of tactility, relegating ideas of physical touch to the affective, emotional realm. As Susan D. Harvey has thoughtfully argued, "one of touch's discursive transpositions mimics this civilizing trend: in the same way that physical impulses are curbed and directed inward, so does tactility become, in addition to the more obvious physiological responses, 'feeling'—the emotional desires and urges that are presented in explicitly physical terms in the early modern iconography of touch." Lincoln demonstrated this association between physical touching, interior feeling, and humanitarianism in his thinking about Southern slavery.[38]

We know that from 1854 on, Lincoln "abhorred" slavery. While the origin of this dislike is admittedly murky, understanding Lincoln's sense of touch and his beliefs about skin helps us fathom the beginnings and evolution of Lincoln's antislavery sentiment.[39] Skin—and not just its color—informed the core of Lincoln's humanitarian sensibility. His tactile understanding of slavery took a couple of forms. For example, Lincoln tended to read freedom—especially the right to the reward of one's labor— haptically. He was fond of invoking the "sweat of thy brow" metaphor. In response to Frederick A. Ross's theological proslavery defense, he wrote, in 1858, "So, at last, it comes to this, that Dr. Ross is to decide the question. And while he consider[s] it, he sits in the shade, with gloves on his hands, and subsists on the bread that Sambo is earning in the burning sun." Hands, heat, burning skin, rough skin: these were his emphases. "When I see strong hands sowing, reaping, and threshing wheat and those same hands grinding and making that wheat into bread," Lincoln commented, "I cannot refrain from wishing . . . that those same hands some way . . . shall own the mouth they feed." Lincoln injected hapticity into the prevailing "fruits of labor" metaphor that guided so much US thinking on the desirability and dignity of free labor.[40]

Questions of ownership mediated by touch were also at play here. Touch was central to eighteenth- and nineteenth-century ideas of possession; the right to touch conveyed ownership and carried all sorts of gender and class implications. In his first annual message to Congress, Lincoln said, pointedly, "no men living are more worthy to be trusted than those who toil up from poverty—none less inclined to take, or touch, aught they have not honestly earned." Slavery was reprehensible because the slaveholders' touch of the slaves' skin, the whippings Lincoln had witnessed as a young man, laid a claim to ownership that was wholly illegitimate and because the enslaved toiled with their hands and had their skin exposed to harsh elements. But the enslaved person's touch did not realize possession, denied as it was by the protocols of Southern slaveholding society.⁴¹

After his assassination in 1865, postbellum iterations kept Lincoln as a "skin-man" alive. His "rugged, wondrous traits" were profiled in popular magazines. In the late 1860s, some artists were not "afraid" of trying to capture Lincoln's "homeliness," and *Harper's Weekly* singled out W. E. Marshall's portrait for endeavoring to capture his "rugged" features. When "first elected president of the United States," Lincoln was described, in some retrospectives, as "raw-boned," with a "shapeless skeleton in a tough, very dirty, unwholesome skin," a description usually reserved for the enslaved.⁴²

But postbellum interest in Lincoln's rough skin was gradually eclipsed by a new understanding of Lincoln, one that stressed a softer-skinned president. Within a few years of his death, the predominant understanding of Lincoln toned down his skin's texture and smoothed over his lines to render him sober, polished, and statesmanlike. Rough, democratic Lincoln was reconstituted as haptically and emotionally bourgeois, a smooth national leader with refined "feelings," a man increasingly touched emotionally but untouching and, importantly, untouchable.⁴³

For example, almost immediately after his death, Lincoln's rough, strong, tough hands became "gentle" at precisely the same time as he was softened and made "moderate" and "loving." He was "the great, good, gentle President Lincoln," a man "moved to tears" by songs, a man of refined character who, by some accounts of the 1870s, was possessed of "gentle and genial manners." By the 1890s, his was a "meek, gentle, tranquil spirit."⁴⁴ So too with his face. An engraving of Lincoln that adorned the front cover of *Harper's Magazine* in April 1885 was criticized for "giving an incorrect idea of Mr. Lincoln's face, the skin of which was smooth, not rough, as one might think from this portrait."[45]

Of course, manipulating images, "likenesses," and daguerre-otypes was common practice in the antebellum period. Individuals who tried to reveal their authentic selves, their inner essences, sometimes found their images shaped and tinkered with. The postbellum manipulation of Lincoln's image echoed this process. Well into the twentieth century, Lincoln's antebellum image was tweaked, his skin softened and rendered gentle and genteel. The new Lincoln was more palatable to an emerging bourgeoisie as a symbol of national identity, one dissociated from the dangerous democratic spirit of the early postbellum periods. Fears of tramps, hoboes, and the propertyless haunted postbellum bourgeois visions of an unbridled American democracy. The new Lincoln iconography countered such rough-and-ready, democratic sentiment by fixing him as a statesmanlike, gentle, and refined national leader. In the process, the experiential aspect of democracy was redefined from something raw and boisterous into a process that was orderly, contained, and safe.[46] Efforts to reconstitute Lincoln as seen and smooth rather than haptic and touchable were central to such a remodeling.

And that remodeling was quite literal, expressed most obviously in sculpture and statuary, the most tactile of art forms. Elites considered the 1931 "sculptured representation of the young Lincoln," designed by Lee Lawrie and carved "in the stone of the Nebraska state capitol," ideal. In the absence of photographs of Lincoln as a young man, Lawrie invented him. For this, Lawrie relied not on the gritty, skin-shriveled biographical descriptions of earlier observers but, rather, on photographs and the mask of Lincoln's face made by Leonard W. Volk in 1860. To capture Lincoln's "early manhood," said Lawrie, "was principally a matter of removing the wrinkles that came with age and worry." But removing Lincoln's wrinkles also served to locate him within a more refined, bourgeois aesthetic. In effect, Lawrie redefined Lincoln by reworking his skin. Gone was the rugged, frontier hide of the young Lincoln, the boy exposed to numbing, skin-sculpting elements, whose skin was invariably described as withered and tanned. Gone, in other words, was a man whose touch was just a bit too common for new bourgeois tastes.[47]

Lincoln's laboring past was not erased entirely. There was too much invested and embedded in it. But his frontiering, rough ways were diluted by postbellum constructions of Lincoln the thinker, the eye-man. Lawrie had the sculpture hold both an axe and a book, for example. It was this braiding of Lincoln the seer and thinker with Lincoln the feeler and doer that had been most successful and best received—and the one that endured in most bronzes and sculptures. The Lincoln Memorial, dedicated in 1922, certainly laced the two "in the action of the hands and the expression of the face." But if artists were ever in doubt which characteristic to stress, Lincoln the thinker, the book-man, the eye-man seemed safest; this aspect secured him as more sophisticated and intellectual. Augustus Saint-Gaudens's 1887 Lincoln Park bronze in Chicago was well loved not least because it was genteel and presented a well-groomed and simply more "presidential" Lincoln.[48]

By contrast, George Grey Barnard's "gaunt and rugged conception of Lincoln as a raw-boned westerner," erected in Cincinnati's Lytle Park in 1917, proved controversial precisely because Barnard profiled Lincoln's skin, highlighting its roughness and hardness, stressing the size of his head and hands, and even making his bones apparent through his clothes. For some, Barnard's unapologetically haptic work depicted Lincoln as a "hobo" and a "slouch" and was therefore a "lie," a "deformed" image that reflected "neither body nor soul" and masked his true "character." The extraordinary roughness of the clothing and the skin was "an insult to the American people and a thwarting of Democracy." Tactile roughness as authenticator of republican simplicity and virtue was evaporating as Lincoln's "true" relationship to democracy was being recast—literally—in papery, vellum-like skin, less gaunt and wizened hands and face, and fitted and comfortable clothes. Lincoln's inner character and the skin that communicated it were smoother than any pre–Civil War image had it.[49]

Not only was Lincoln made to look less rugged in several sculptures, but he was usually placed well out of arm's—and hand's—reach. For example, Lawrie's work on the Nebraska State Capitol looked "down on the city that bears his name from a height of about 150 feet." The Union Square statue of Lincoln in New York City, erected in 1870, was also virtually untouchable: it stood "on a granite pedestal, twenty-two feet high."[50] So too with the Lincoln Memorial. Its smooth, marble figure is cordoned off, untouchable, and on a pedestal ten feet high. And the Freedmen's Memorial Monument in Lincoln Park, Washington, DC, erected in 1876 and roundly criticized by Frederick Douglass for depicting Lincoln emancipating a kneeling slave, is also revealing. Indeed, Lincoln does not touch the body of the freedman; his only tactile engagement is with his right hand on the Emancipation Proclamation. His left hand hovers over the formerly enslaved man's head. Given the importance African Americans attached to Lincoln's emancipatory touch just after the war, this hands-off gesture is telling. "I know I am free," exclaimed an ex-slave in Richmond, having seen Lincoln escorted through the streets, "for I have seen Father Abraham and felt him."[51] But that touch was not captured in the monument. Even at its founding, the Freedmen's Memorial Monument was contested—and hands, images of touching and not touching, and, ultimately, who had the right to touch whom, and what, were important to that discussion.

Placing Lincoln beyond the hands of the masses reaffirmed his burgeoning visual status (at the expense of his tactility), and, set up so high, Lincoln became the quintessential expression of the bourgeois image. He looked down, or out, beyond reach of the great unwashed. Distancing in this fashion was hardly new. According to Peter Stallybrass and Allon White, nineteenth-century British elites understood the working class, many of whom lived too close for physical comfort, as couriers of coarse manners and disease. Their presence rendered the nineteenth-century English bourgeoisie a nervous bunch who managed to at once avoid touching the masses and maintain a watchful eye on their activities by viewing them, out of reach, from balconies. In part, distancing Lincoln was also part of another cultural process in which artifacts were increasingly rendered more visual and less touchable. As Constance Classen and David Howes have shown, the resolutely visualist aesthetic and protocols of nineteenth- and twentieth-century British museums in which patrons were urged to look at, not touch, artifacts were relatively new developments. Prior to the nineteenth century, visitors to museums were encouraged to touch items: feeling the weight and texture of an object conferred authenticity on the artifact and, curators believed, helped visitors appreciate the past more reliably than seeing alone allowed. To be sure, visitors were elites and their touch was considered suitably delicate, but the idea that only owners of artifacts could touch them was alien. Only with the rise of the public museum did touch and ownership become braided; the injunction to look but not touch was considered increasingly necessary to protect artifacts from the mucky, laboring hands of the hoi polloi.[52]

Given this context, the very few touchable Lincoln statues proved controversial. Gutzon Borglum's "utterly original" statue of Lincoln in Newark, New Jersey (1917) famously has him sitting wearily on a park bench. Children from the neighborhood loved climbing on the statue, which is precisely why Lincoln's son Robert hated it: it could be touched by working-class children and "used as a playground by the hoodlum children of the neighborhood." Moreover, Borglum, like Barnard, depicted Lincoln as rugged, his skin heavily textured. It was no accident that Borglum's sitting Lincoln in Newark and his massive bronze bust at the Lincoln Tomb in Springfield emphasized his rugged skin and were designed to be touched directly by the public. So was Barnard's Cincinnati statue. His "haggard-looking Lincoln" was "practically at ground level," according to Albert Boime.[53]

Despite all of this, Lincoln's skin stays with us, lingering in quiet but important ways. He can still be touched, on a daily basis, in fact. Americans find him in their pockets, not on a five-dollar bill—that's the visual, flat, linear Lincoln. Instead, Lincoln is felt on the ubiquitous penny. True, time and rubbing have probably left a smooth Lincoln between the fingers, but feel carefully and one will detect in coppery relief his hair and features. In the absence of lower pedestals or statues capturing his textured skin, it is one of the few ways left to get in touch with Abraham Lincoln.

This, in turn, raises pressing interpretive issues about Lincoln's lingering touch in monuments—whom he touches, whom he does not touch, and why. Insistent and deeply ingrained attitudes about race have shaped the way Americans have understood Lincoln's touch. When alive, he glad-handed often, but those hands were almost exclusively white and masculine. The demands of our own time, notably the renewed call for racial justice most closely associated with the Black Lives Matter (BLM) movement, have raised key interpretive and political questions about not only how to touch Lincoln but also whether his tactile appearance is still "in touch," is still relevant, especially in the United States. While BLM and associated movements have understandably called for—and helped actively dismantle—Confederate monuments that litter the modern American landscape (keep in mind that the vast majority of these monuments were erected long after the end of the Civil War for the express purpose of celebrating and enacting continued racial subordination), what has puzzled some observers is the critique leveled against Lincoln memorials and statuary. But a careful appreciation of the history of tactility in the United States, especially its racial history and Lincoln's place in it, helps us make better sense of that critique.

Take, for example, the aforementioned Freedmen's Memorial Monument. Recent arguments in favor of reworking and reimagining the monument make the case that although it was paid for by formerly enslaved people, it was designed by Thomas Ball, a white man, without their input, and that the statue reinforces the white narrative that Lincoln freed the slaves and ignores the contributions of millions of African Americans in forcing the Union to make the Civil War one about slavery and not just one about the preservation of the Union (a point Frederick Douglass stressed in his dedication address). To this, add the history of tactility. Lincoln's touch had always been framed within the coordinates of white American men—they were his constituents. In the Freedmen's Memorial Monument, Lincoln does not touch the kneeling freedman, thereby reinscribing the (racialized) distance between white emancipator and Black freedman. There is no handshaking in this monument; that would have connoted racial equality. The Freedmen's Memorial Monument places Lincoln out of touch not just of viewers but of the very subject—the formerly enslaved man—who is kneeling at Lincoln's feet. There is no hint of tactile engagement in the design and no indication of the very thing for which Lincoln was lauded by white America: his in-touch quality. It is hardly surprising, then, that for many modern viewers, the monument reeks of racialized distancing. Even in freedom, the Black man does not touch the great (white) Emancipator. Given the abiding, fraught, and disconcerting history of racialized touch in the United States—a history defined by slavery's ability to grant whites the freedom to violently touch, at will, Black bodies; a history that actively promoted the tactile distancing between white and Black under segregation, where Blacks were deemed "untouchable" except in instances of brute violence—it is easier to understand why even casual viewers of the monument find something unsettling and offensive about Thomas Ball's creation. It is, simply put, invested with a racialized history of tactility.[54]

The point I wish to stress here is simple: structural shifts in sensory environments, changes in sensory perceptions and habits, shifts in the ways the senses were (and are) produced and consumed were (and are) not merely incidental to key historical developments but constitutive of them. Sounds, smells, tastes, sights, and touches can certainly reflect larger developments—such as modernization, industrialization, the rise of a particular form of political economy—but they can also help constitute and define those developments. Not attending to the sensory presence in these developments impoverishes our understanding of their texture, denies us access to understanding how and why structures and perceptions emerged and changed as they did, and unhelpfully reinscribes long-held conceits about class, gender, and race. Sounds, smells, and touches did not simply reflect social realities but also assumed an agency in making them. The senses, as the above examples show, shaped identities, functioned to animate and create power structures, and served to give specific shape to forms of protest, animate emotion, and inform memory. In short, a history without the senses is a history very partially told, and a potentially hazardous one at that.

# CHAPTER 3

# Future

## Paths Possible

One reason for the success of sensory history—notably, its ability to migrate into multiple subfields and populate the study of many geographies and eras—also explains why its future, at least in terms of areas and topics of possible investigation, is necessarily murky. Precisely because of the field's enormous geographic and temporal reach, any discussion of the future of sensory history is necessarily an exercise in vague prognostication. While prediction is difficult and, frankly, not terribly important (for the trajectories will evolve as they will, regardless of what I write here), and while there are other, more timely ways to access what is going on in the field, it is helpful to at least gesture toward what might prove fruitful avenues of future inquiry.[1]

It is worth asking some basic questions and proffering some possible answers. Which topics could sensory historians investigate with profit? What are some of the emerging themes in the field? This chapter offers, albeit in highly preliminary form, some suggestions. I wish here to do more than simply enumerate possible topics for analysis and areas of inquiry (although, of necessity, there's some of that). After all, we already possess powerful and persuasive calls for identifying valuable trajectories of sensory studies generally. For example, as David Howes and others have properly argued, we simply must attend much more to intersensoriality and synesthesia—the relationship among the senses—if we are to understand the true breadth and depth of the historical sensorium.[2]

It is also worth asking *how* the history of the senses could be written in the future. Should it continue on its same trajectory, with books dedicated to each sense and multisensory analyses? Or should we think of embedding the senses more thoroughly into existing narratives, as some of the earliest sensory historians did? Mark S. R. Jenner has argued that we need to do the latter. Jenner rightly insists that we should not treat the history of the senses in a zero-sum fashion—that we should not assume a dilution of one sense necessarily means an elevation of another—and suggests that we should think in terms of sensory multiplicities. Jenner seems to be calling for a more integrated sensory history, one that does not artificially extract a sense from its context but understands it in the larger context in which it existed and pays particular attention to how various senses and sensory habits interacted. There is much to recommend these points. Yet in order to integrate the history of smell, say, into a historical narrative and to understand how, for example, olfaction connected to taste, we need the hard work of olfactory historical excavation, and that is sometimes best achieved through a dedicated, focused history of smell and smelling.[3]

Possible future topics and subjects are many. Some topics, once examined, are now due for a reconsideration. For example, despite the pioneering work by Bernard Hibbits on the senses and the law, much remains to be done on how the sensate has inflected legal discourse, proceedings, and conclusions.[4] Other recent work has reminded us of the importance of silence as a form of political protest, and it is also increasingly apparent that sound itself cannot properly be understood unless we think of it as constituted, at least in part, by silence(s). Still other work, such as on the sensory and emotional history of sport, offers genuinely new insight and a fecund platform for further growth.[5]

We will also need to attend more to a broader variety of sensory constituencies. Plainly, more work needs to be done on the sensory construction of race and, especially, gender. On gender, we would do well to think carefully about sensory histories of the LGBTQ+ community as well as standard male/female sensory constructions. Age also matters. Do the senses evolve over time and, if so, to what extent are sensory regimens and habits shaped by age (itself a culturally constructed category)? Are sensory histories of the elderly the same as those of children? Similarly, we will also see greater sensitivity to the senses and disabilities. Here, disability studies can be woven into sensory history with precision and help flesh out even very new areas of inquiry. Any study of aging should consider the link between anosmia and dementia, for example. It is also worth remembering, as Mara Mills has pointed out, that sensory disabilities have impacted mainstream society: audiobooks, commercialized after increased blindness courtesy of World War II, have contributed to the reauralization of reading habits.[6] Neither should sensory history limit itself to humans. Animal studies, an already vibrant subfield of historical inquiry, seems ideally suited to a sensory historical analysis, one in which humans take their material and metaphorical sensory cues from animals' smells, sounds, touches; where historians can examine how humans attempted to understand the sensory history of animals themselves; and where the senses served to define human-animal relations.[7]

Whatever the specific topics, places, and times historians of the senses will explore, they will likely do so in a way that transcends categories in a very deliberate fashion. By this I mean that established categories of, for example, time and era (medieval, modern, and the like) will continue to attract attention but will also invite greater scrutiny. Temporal bookends will become more plastic and less definite not least because the study of the senses helps redefine conventional temporalities.

Indeed, historians of the senses have begun to think about how sensory experience tends to muddle periodization and conventional historical eras. Peter Denney, Bruce Buchan, David Ellison, and Karen Crawley's 2019 edited collection of essays, *Sound, Space and Civility in the British World, 1700–1850*, serves as a powerful reminder that sensory history does not lend itself terribly well to conventional historical periodization partly because it often charts the *longue durée* and partly because sensory changes and perceptions of sensory changes were often slow, incremental, and intermittent, with echoes from earlier periods lingering and braiding with new sensory stimuli and modes of perception in often quiet, subtle fashion. Despite the manifest cultural and technological changes apparent in the period 1700–1850, the debates over noise and sound, listening and hearing, detailed by the essays in the collection were part of a much longer trajectory. As several scholars of the early modern period and even before—including the medieval and ancient world—have shown, discussions about who was noisy and who was "sound" were driven by elites for hundreds of years, with social standing mattering a great deal in designating who was noisy (and noisome) and who understood the intellectual propriety of silence and modulated sound. The period from roughly 1700 to 1850 is difficult to characterize sensorially simply because many of the tensions apparent in that period had existed, albeit in germinated form with different constituencies, much earlier.[8]

Sensory history's heavy emphasis on cultural, social, and intellectual history needs to be supplemented if we are to make better sense of this reperiodization. Scholars of political economy should be actively invited to bring to bear their expertise on how to make better sense of any period, the modern one especially. Indeed, if we reframe the history of the senses generally in terms of political economy, the period 1700–1850 begins to make better sense. This is the era of classical political economy, a period when state intervention into the public sphere to regulate noise and sound was present but, compared to later years, quite modest. The 1850 cutoff also makes good sense, at least in the Anglo-American world, because it serves as a precursor to the rise of another form of political economy, one centered on greater state intervention. In Anglo-America, this is the period of progressivism, when local municipalities especially began to exert greater control over the definition of noisemaking.[9]

Although we certainly need more work on twentieth-century soundscapes (and the senses generally), especially for the post-1945 period and most especially for the very recent era, with the rise of so-called neoliberalism and the associated retreat from state regulation (usually dated as beginning in the 1980s), it seems like a safe guess that the rise of manifest state intervention in Western European countries between and after the two world wars was likely reflected in the ways that government increasingly attempted to control the modern soundscape, especially with regard to traffic, industry, and noise pollution in the skies. The precise nature of the connection demands much more detailed analysis (not to mention the pressing need for interrogation of the relationship between neoliberalism and very late twentieth-century political economies). But it might well be the case that rather than index the history of the senses generally to extant and quite finely sliced periodizations (Enlightenment, industrialization, and the like), we could equally talk about the political economy of the senses in broader terms.

If sensory history generally holds the potential to reperiodize historical eras or, at least, allows us to think differently about how to periodize, it seems likely that the long-term trend toward the rejection and redefinition of the Great Divide theory will continue in writing on the senses. While this theory, most closely associated with Marshall McLuhan and Walter Ong, was more subtle than some interpretations allow, it did nevertheless make the case for the elevation of the eye to the preeminent sense of truth and knowledge during the long Enlightenment and strongly suggested that the senses of hearing, olfaction, taste, touch, and even intuition (a sort of common sense that had been taken seriously in the ancient and medieval world) not only were less reliable when it came to establishing truth but should also be abandoned entirely, because they were inconsistent with science and reason (as was the case with intuition). If sensory history has taught us anything, it is that the Enlightenment did not elevate sight to the utter excision of the other senses and that the nonvisual senses were not only important to key developments in the modern world but constitutive of them. Indeed, I think it fair to say that the writing of sensory history now consistently and correctly challenges the central point of the Great Divide theory—the idea that the Enlightenment elevated sight and downplayed the other senses to the point of only nominal relevance. Given that this tendency will doubtless continue, I suspect we will see, and properly so, work on both the continued relevance of so-called forgotten senses, such as intuition (through an analysis of various sixth senses, including spiritual perception and psychophysics), in the post-Enlightenment era and more work devoted to the modern era, especially for the post–World War II period. We already possess helpful signposts. Joy Parr's magnificent and certainly groundbreaking study on the sensory impact and experience of Canadian megaprojects (including large dam construction, the building of nuclear plants, and the establishment of military bases) details the period 1953–2003. I believe Parr's book is, chronologically at least, among the most recent analyses of the modern period generally. Focusing on this period offers many dividends to the sensory historian. The sheer scale of late twentieth-century industrial development offers us a unique opportunity to understand sensory limits and the ways in which peoples' senses were not only made but remade by huge environmental change. And as Parr also shows, some of these environmental changes courted environmental disasters not always detectable by the senses. Tainted water eluded the eye, nose, and tongue and called into question the very reliability of the modern human sensorium. Plainly, whatever the particulars of the post–World War II era, this work shows that it is no longer helpful to think of the Enlightenment as a moment in which the nonvisual senses were eclipsed in favor of the eye.[10]

If sensory history has both reworked historians' sense of time and promises to continue to expand temporalities, the same may be said of its effects on space. To date, the bulk of work on the history of the senses has been framed around discrete geographies, albeit the history of the nation-state or specific cities and regions. Such a geographic focus has been immensely helpful. It has allowed us access to specifically urban sensory histories, granted us comparisons of rural and urban soundscapes (and, courtesy of work on ports, seascapes); it has helped us think in terms of national sensory identities across a range of societies over any number of eras. Much-needed and very recent work on, for example, the historical acoustemology of modern

Egypt is most welcome and offers an exceptionally useful counterweight to what is a very pronounced emphasis on Western European and US history in the field, but even this frames its subject matter within the coordinates of the nation-state.[11]

The emphasis on regional and national sensory histories is not without merit, not least because it has, in fact, helped historians move beyond borders by providing deep empirical work with which to offer either comparison or analyses of sensory migrations. Very recent work suggests that new ways of thinking about the senses and space, the senses and geographies, will move beyond the confines of the nation-state and specific regions and tackle the senses in new ways. This is entirely fitting to the intellectual impetus behind sensory history, after all: since the field is dedicated to excavating how and why the senses are historically and culturally constructed, sensory historians are under some obligation to similarly interrogate the historical construction of their investigative categories, such as the nation-state. The dividends here are evident in recent work. For example, Andrew Kettler's pathbreaking study, *The Smell of Slavery: Olfactory Racism and the Atlantic World*, deliberately places the senses into a framework stressing migration and exchange. Kettler skillfully explores how European and English olfactory practices and stereotypes were redeployed in the New World to instigate racial thinking and write the tactics of racial subordination that accompanied that thinking. He is careful to examine exchanges between white colonial settlers, Native Americans, and enslaved West Africans, pointing to the material properties of smell as well as to the intellectual categories that anchored olfactory stereotypes. Importantly, he remains alert to how olfaction generated within nation-states and religious identities evolved in the context of massive transatlantic migration and engagement. A similar dividend is apparent in Andrew J. Rotter's exceptional study of the senses and imperialism. Rotter's *Empires of the*

*Senses: Bodily Encounters in Imperial India and the Philippines*
takes the nation-state as its basis (in this case, Britain and the
United States) and examines how sensory stereotypes and sensory experiences were exported to and influenced colonizers and
colonists in India and the Philippines. Rotter pays close attention
to how colonized land smelled, felt, sounded, looked, and tasted
to imperial adventurers and examines how colonizers were in
turn influenced by the sensory worlds they attempted to claim
and the inhabitants they essayed to control. There are sober-
ing tales of the limits of sensory dominion in both Kettler's and
Rotter's works; there is also a clear case to be made that unless
we think of the senses as migratory, indexed to and shaped by
movement and encounter, we will necessarily end up limiting
how we understand sensory change and evolution, geographi-
cally and culturally.[12]

The senses, then, can be untethered from strict geographi-
cal confines; they can also be altered, stretched, and redefined in
relatively short periods of time. Evidence of this sensory plas-
ticity, at least historically, can be found in two largely under-
studied areas: the history of environmental disasters and the
curiously underexamined sensory history of wars and armed
conflicts. It seems to me that there are two main dividends to
studying wars and environmental disasters from a sensory-his-
tory perspective. First, wars and environmental disasters not
only heighten, deaden, and stretch the senses but also create a
sensory recognition that smells and touches and sounds assume
much greater salience than they do under "ordinary" conditions.
As Alexis Peri has poignantly shown, World War II, notably the
siege of Leningrad, rearranged the senses. The siege animated
the sense of taste, for example, while diluting vision in both the
short and the long term. Indeed, wars—especially modern industrial ones—seem to share certain sensory signatures. They often
muddle the certainty of vision, possess a certain atavistic quality

(whereby the presumed lower senses of smell, touch, and taste take on much greater significance than conventional, preexisting sensory protocols typically permit), take on an unusual volume and intensity, and linger long after the moment has passed.[13]

The environment generally, when under duress, similarly stretches and rearranges the senses. As Joy Parr has shown, local knowledge, especially in the little-studied post–World War II period, was both embodied in and mediated through the senses. Mega construction projects and responses to the outbreaks of diseases (notably the *E. coli* outbreak in Walkerton, Ontario, in 2001) showed how the senses were placed under strain and were often unable to function as reliable sentinels or as sources of knowledge. Environmental disasters have had similar effects. As a limited but growing body of work on this subject shows, disasters, from hurricanes to tsunamis, occur in a particular context and not only shape the social, political, and economic conditions in which they occur but also alter and manipulate the senses. These events are processed and experienced sensorially at the time (the sounds of hurricanes, for example, are preeminent) and shape the way people recover from (and remember) disasters. More than that, the way people experience disasters sensorially and, more precisely, the way they communicate about them can impact structures we conventionally do not think of as having sensory resonance. For example, a good case can be made that the sensory experience of hurricanes, earthquakes, and tsunamis in the Danish West Indies in the year 1867—and the way that people expressed their emotional and physical experience of these disasters sensorially—impacted decisions in the US State Department and the very nature of US foreign policy. Arguably, the United States decided not to acquire these Danish territories in that year because of the way that residents and officials described the experience of the hurricanes, earthquakes, and tsunamis. They did so in highly sensory terms that deterred US diplomats from aggressively pursuing the appropriation of a place that they felt they had no ability to control. Howling hurricanes, skin-scraping earthquakes, and stench-inducing tsunamis all rearranged the sensory hierarchy, demoted vision, and lent the Danish West Indies, in the opinion of both inhabitants and US diplomats, an untamable quality: sensorially, the place was capricious, unpredictable, and a direct challenge to the stable nineteenth-century sensorium they had come to enjoy. Here, the senses functioned in a causal way, affecting US foreign policy, as well as in an existential fashion, mediating the way in which people experienced environmental disasters.[14] It bears noting here, too, that sensory histories of natural disasters, especially of environmental disasters such as hurricanes, might well lead to a more robust understanding of climate change and how it has been experienced sensorially.

A second benefit of studying sensory extremes, or the senses under extreme circumstances, is that such an approach reveals with precision the historical irreproducibility of the senses. The sensory experience of war or hurricanes or tsunamis cannot be reproduced—not simply because of the scale and capriciousness of these events but because, as with all other sensory experiences, they occur in context. The smell of thousands of dead bodies, human and animal, for example, cannot (and, ethically, should not) be reproduced or reconsumed. The ways in which the senses functioned in war and under duress point to the utter need for a contextual reading of sensory evidence.[15]

## Interdisciplinarity

Beyond enumerating new areas of possible inquiry, I want to discuss not just the "what" of sensory history's future but the "how": how the field might develop and refine itself epistemologically, interpretively, and historiographically.

Since its inception, sensory history has been a product of gestures toward interdisciplinarity (recall, for example, Huizinga's early work). Thanks to the contributions of sensory studies, which deliberately draws on multiple disciplines, this is likely to continue—and profitably, too. Disciplinary boundaries within subfields are especially plastic. Take, for example, the relationship between historical acoustemology and musicology. Certainly, there has been (and continues to be) a certain wariness between the fields of sound studies and musicology. As Alejandra Bronfman and Christine Ehrick comment, "Latin America can often be fetishized through music, both in and outside the region. More than perhaps we realize, the neocolonial gaze on Latin America has long had a strong aural component."[16] This might help explain why the initial historical study of sound and listening tended to write its own trajectory, veering away from the history of music. But important recent work suggests that the two fields are beginning to converse. As Josephine Hoegaerts and Kaarina Kilpiö have argued, cultural musicologists and sound historians are natural allies when it comes to making sense of sounds past. With careful contextualization guiding the research of both sound studies scholars and cultural musicologists, Hoegaerts and Kilpiö insist that historical acoustemology can be profitably served if we marry what Jonathan Sterne has called the "paper trail" left by sound reproduction technologies with the historian's "experience with dust and the archival void of past lives." Written representations of sounds, silences, and listening habits, they properly argue, can helpfully augment sounds made available to us through recorded technology, provided we contextualize both types of source. "If one conclusion can be arrived at," Hoegaerts and Kilpiö maintain, "it is perhaps that such a cross-disciplinary approach to sounds of the past remains a matter of historicization."[17]

Sound studies has tended, sometimes for legitimate reasons, to exclude music or at least minimize its importance. Some race theorists worry that profiling music too highly serves to stereotype racially constructed habits of listening, and they have offered useful ways of rethinking music to avoid the trap of racial reinscription. Jennifer Lynn Stoever has sensibly suggested that understanding the racial construction of sound—the sonic color line, as she calls it—"should compel scholars to question music's cultural and institutional privilege rather than assuming it." Instead, she helpfully recommends "rearticulating music as a culturally and historically conditioned form of sound in political relation to (and flowing from, and toward) other sounds."[18] To be sure, music still—rightly, in my estimation—occupies an important space in the writing of historical acoustemology, but I think future studies (with Stoever's wise counsel in mind) need to make a more concerted effort to reintegrate music into the historical soundscape in an effort to constitute music as one set of sounds among many, very much along the lines of J. Martin Daughtry's *Listening to War: Sound, Music, Trauma, and Survival in Wartime Iraq* or, more recently, Nicholas Hammond's *The Powers of Sound and Song in Early Modern Paris.*[19]

There are, of course, many ways in which sensory history could take up insights and techniques from other fields and disciplines to advance its cause. Careful and continued borrowing from literature, for example, is welcome, as is a renewed commitment by scholars of literature to the sensate. Scholars of literature have much to offer here. Historians are sometimes hesitant to borrow heavily from literature in their search for sensory evidence, not least because such evidence can court a presentist or ahistorical conceit, one in which the sounds of the past serve largely to animate the present without the sort of heavy contextualization historians usually demand. Clearly, this is not to say that literary evidence—or, for that matter, sensory history work by scholars of literature—cannot properly historicize its subjects. Literary senses can be fully historicized, as Hans Rindisbacher showed in his fine 1992 study, *The Smell of Books*.[20]

Lastly, I think it is also worth pointing to very recent efforts by historians of the senses and historians of emotion to bring their respective fields into closer dialogue. There is, after all, a deep, if often ignored, genealogy linking the history of emotion with the history of the senses and emotion. Huizinga gestured toward it; Febvre and Mandrou were explicit about it; Corbin called for it. This early work called for a deeper exploration of the connection between the two and, while that call has been largely forgotten, it seems as though the challenges faced by each field might in part be solved through greater collaboration. Upon considered reflection, few historians of the senses would claim that they can reliably study the senses without attending to their emotional content, and vice versa. Such collaboration might also have unexpected dividends, including a closer engagement with the natural sciences, notably social psychology and neurology. Plainly, historical research dedicated to just the senses or emotions will continue, and this is appropriate. We will continue to benefit from discrete studies of various emotions and senses in particular contexts. But alongside that specialized work, historians of emotions and of the senses will increasingly need to read one another's work with care simply to better understand why, say, a particular sensory habit or emotional register emerged at a particular time in a given way. We need to better appreciate the entanglement of the senses and the emotions, and that understanding is most likely to emerge if a sustained dialogue between the two fields is established and cultivated.[21]

## How

Earlier, I discussed the rapid increase in production in historical writing on the senses at some length because I think it highlights a point central to this manifesto. It seems to me that a good deal of this work emerged and is emerging so quickly in a context of relative (although sometimes exaggerated) freshness and disciplinary newness that discussion of the larger interpretive issues at stake in the writing of sensory history can sometimes be elided, poorly attended to, or even ignored. I say this not necessarily by way of criticism of individual works but as a commentary on the state of the field. In other words, sensory historians are producing more books and articles than ever on sensory history; we are expanding our empirical reach to include constituencies previously excluded; and we are doing so in a roiling, additive fashion that is making the field more popular than ever. But what we are not doing as much is arguing among ourselves about things that any field must discuss: methodology, how to read sources, and the interpretive stakes in doing sensory history. So much work has been produced so quickly that the field generally is no longer emerging: it has emerged. And this fact makes the stakes even greater, because an already established field can be susceptible to ossification or prone to lapse into happy complacency in the absence of critique and rigorous argument.[22]

I do not wish to be misunderstood. I am not asking for internecine warfare among sensory historians. I like our collegiality and I admire our remarkably supportive environment.[23] What I am asking for is rather more mutual interrogation of our work and, frankly, historians of the senses are probably the best positioned to undertake those conversations. Should we not, I worry about how well the field will mature, how it will refine itself, and whether it will slip into easy self-congratulation of the sort that inspires quiet complacency.

If we are to think creatively and carefully about how to write sensory history, we would do well to look to some of the early work discussed in chapter 1 by way of example. Some of it, replete with its competing interpretive and methodological claims, remains relevant and, I think, is well worth remembering as we think about the current and future state of the field. Some of the early practitioners of sensory history were precisely those who favored debate, invited sometimes pointed scholarly conversation, and embraced the kind of constructive criticism for which I am calling here. If historical approaches to writing about the senses were worth debating several decades ago, they are worth debating now, too, and some of those debates hold value for the future writing of sensory history.

I am thinking here of some of Alain Corbin's interventions into the field of sensory history that were not only empirical but also, and importantly, interpretive and methodological.[24] Corbin's counsel was, simply, that despite the manifest dividends of sensory history, it must be willing to research not just the history of smell, sound, touch, touch, sight, and taste; it must also pay particular attention to method and be willing to engage in constructive criticism. This is fundamentally the point I wish to stress. Healthy challenges, disagreements, interventions: all are essential to helping us remain alert to interpretive pitfalls and slippery false starts.

Particular senses have benefited from robust debate. From quite early on, for example, historians of olfaction have been willing to challenge one another. Arguably, Corbin himself set the tone by showing a happy willingness to engage. And despite Corbin's preeminence in the field, Mark S. R. Jenner has helpfully challenged Corbin's interpretation in robust and often constructive fashion. In 2000, Jenner correctly identified Corbin as "indubitably the pioneer" of the cultural history of smell but considered his arguments and chronology unsystematic and "misguided." Specifically, not only does Jenner think it unhelpful to isolate the study of smell ("experience is fundamentally synesthetic," he says), but he also finds framing "research in terms of whether there was a fundamental sensory transformation, a shift from an odoriphile to an odoriphobe culture . . . an unhelpfully crude way of approaching the cultural history of the senses and of scents." Jenner continues: "Nor, furthermore, are odours banished altogether. One odour can be decried while another is celebrated and cherished. It is surely more productive to begin to trace a history of smells, exploring the cultural meanings of particular odours in specific locations or within particular discourses, rather than a history of smell."[25] Jenner's point is not without merit. As Jonathan Reinarz has recently argued, historians of olfaction are increasingly concerned to disrupt established and unhelpful interpretive binaries currently defining the field (foul versus fragrant, for example) by reconceptualizing smell as far more varied, subtle, and even intersensorial.[26]

Still, such engagement is relatively rare. Despite its deeper genealogy, historical acoustemology, for example, is quite a long way from this sort of critical examination. Because of the comparative dearth of work on touch and taste, historians of those topics would do well to think in terms of critical engagement even as they compile the foundations necessary for the growth of those topics.[27] It is precisely because we care about sensory history that we should not shy away from informed, honest, and constructive criticism. To not do so will impoverish us all and stunt the maturity of arguably one of the most promising fields of historical inquiry to emerge in years.

I am not the only observer to raise this issue. Neil Gregor has expressed similar concerns in his highly favorable but probing 2015 review of Daniel Morat's edited collection, *Sounds of Modern History: Auditory Cultures in 19th- and 20th-Century Europe*. Gregor reminds us that the field of aural history "has been around for a little longer than some would like to imagine," and while he endorses calls for allowing the field to continue along its current lines of intellectual openness and creativity (something I heartily applaud), he adds that "it may also

be time to open up some more explicit polarities in the debate."
"It is," says Gregor, "a necessary part of the process of defining
a field that its early protagonists support each other's explor-
atory moves, but, as the earlier dynamics of emergence of fields
such as gender history showed, there comes a point where some
hitherto submerged disagreements need clearer articulation."
In other words, the field, precisely because it is so important, is
worth arguing over.[28]

Similarly, Ari Y. Kelman has upped the methodological and
theoretical ante in discussions about how to "do" sound history
by highlighting the epistemological and heuristic shortfalls of
the ubiquitous term "soundscapes." Kelman makes the sensible
claim that R. Murray Schafer's original framing of the term was
at once restrictive and often contradictory, and he asserts that
the way scholars from various disciplines (historians included)
have applied the term is now so far removed from Schafer's
application that the notion of soundscapes, while seemingly
indispensable, is also entirely too plastic and lacking in analytic
specificity. For Kelman, Schafer's use of the term is prescriptive
and limiting, more indicative of Schafer's penchant for training listeners than advancing enduring interpretive or methodological value. Kelman shows (convincingly, to my mind) how
the term "soundscape" has proven seductive yet quite limiting,
requiring historians such as Emily Thompson to so redefine the
term as to render the meaning of the word muddled and unclear.
Kelman believes that Schafer's soundscape—which he considers divorced from the habit of listening and highly decontextualized from place and time—bears little similarity to the way
many historians use the term.[29]

In a way, Kelman is quite properly asking how historical
sound studies continues to emerge. Does it mature principally
through the addition of new work, more work, work on people,
places, and times previously unexamined? Yes, of course. But

Kelman also seems to be suggesting that for the field to continue to grow it needs to pay attention to theory and terminol-
ogy, interrogating precisely what we mean with the terms we
deploy.

An additional challenge for the future of sensory history
concerns motivation. Why write the senses into history? One
incentive to include the sensate in historical writing was primarily a literary one, inspired by an effort to animate prose with
references to smells, sounds, and tastes. The idea here, it seems,
was to make history accessible, to appeal to the fabled popular
readership so coveted by commercial and academic presses. The
senses enlivened prose and granted the writing an immediacy, a
vitality, and excitement often very hard to capture in standard
forms of historical writing.[30]

How best to use the senses in historical writing is not a
new question. In his 1929 essay on the writing of cultural history, Huizinga helpfully explained that historians face a particular problem. They are, and often have been, the most accessible
of scholars, and their works can be of popular appeal, holding
the potential to snake into wide circulation. "No other disci-
pline," mused Huizinga, "has its portals so wide open to the general public as history."[31] One way this popularity is achieved is
through the use of sensory language to animate prose.

While historians who sell books numbering in the low hundreds might be shocked by this claim, there is no end of historical works populating the best-seller list. Such books tend
to be of a particular sort. Some aim, in self-aware fashion, to
reach a popular audience, and they sometimes deploy the sensate as one way to reach those eyes and ears. In US historical writing, books on the Civil War are a good example. Here,
some of the best-selling authors have used references to smells,
sounds, tastes, and touches in the context of a bloody war not
really to capture the meaning of those sensory experiences for

the historical actors but, rather, to animate their own prose by attributing, frequently without any evidence whatsoever, what a certain battle or engagement smelled or sounded like.[32]

There are now also important market and bureaucratic forces emerging that will challenge all historians, especially historians of the senses, to make their work more "relevant." In and of itself, "relevance" is not necessarily unhelpful, of course. Historians of the senses should want their work to be read by a wide audience. But when funding mechanisms begin to guide what is written and how, historians must take care not to allow their work to be held hostage to those directives. Motivation matters, and market and political forces that valorize "relevance" for its own sake could well erode the historicity of sensory history. We need reminding of the dangers of this kind of writing lest we end up merely catering to expectations, avoiding our responsibility to educate, and, in essence, surrendering to politically inspired, corporatist-informed, consumer-driven, and bureaucratically enforced calls to make the discipline of history "relevant," a trajectory perfectly evidenced in higher education in the United Kingdom since the mid-1990s (where some granting agencies insist on "relevance" and measurable "impact") as well as in the Netherlands, where some funding bodies insist on "knowledge utilization."[33]

Huizinga anticipated the dangers of such an approach: "Our culture suffers if the writing of history for a broader public falls into the hands of the writers of an aestheticizing, emotional history that stems from a literary need, works with literary means, and aims at literary effects. When we pretend to believe in historical constructions that we know are poetic license we are, at best, like the father in Punch playing with his son's toy. Critical scholarship's the only form for understanding the past which is appropriate to our culture, the only form that is natural to it and is its mature product."[34] Has Huizinga's counsel won out? It is difficult to say, of course, but I think the answer is, in part, yes, at least if we think in terms of scholarly monographs. In other respects, it has not. In the realm of living museums, historic homes, the heritage industry generally, and popular forms of historic reenactment, the answer is far less certain— not least because the market and funding pressures at work here are considerable.

Scholarly monographs have not remained immune to such pressures, and a few seem to have deployed the senses in an effort to appeal to a popular audience. Perhaps the best example is a book published by Beacon (a commercial press) in 2005 by two eminent historians of American slavery, Shane White and Graham White, of the University of Sydney. The book, *The Sounds of Slavery: Discovering African American Thought Through Songs, Sermons, and Speech,* catalogues some of slavery's sounds, mostly musical and linguistic, from the mid-eighteenth century to until just after the abolition of slavery and the end of the US Civil War in 1865. The authors argue that the sounds of African American culture, especially when expressed musically, were distinctive, with roots deep in the enslaved people's West African homelands. These sounds, they maintain, collided with European musical and speech forms. The sounds of "black culture" in the eighteenth and nineteenth centuries alienated whites not least because African American music (and certain types of speech) was nonlinear and mixed. What whites heard as irregular and jarring (noise?), blacks heard as meaningful, vibrant, and rhythmic.

Importantly, the book is accompanied by a compact disc (CD) with eighteen tracks of field calls, prayers, and spirituals that were recorded and collected by folklorists John Lomax and Alan Lomax in the 1930s. Shane White and Graham White use them in an effort to illustrate the meaning of African American sounds.

There are problems with this sort of approach, ones that demand fuller discussion and consideration, especially by sensory historians generally and scholars of historical acoustemology specifically. Most obviously, the inclusion of the CD invites the question: Can recordings from the 1930s reproduce the sounds of slavery? Although the authors claim they "bring us about as close as we are ever going to get to hearing" the sounds of slavery, "our" listening, no matter how earnest, cannot interpret the sounds with the same "meaning" as, say, the ears of enslaved people or those of abolitionists. While the authors acknowledge that we "cannot really recover the sounds" of slavery, they nevertheless invite us, in their text, to listen to particular tracks on the CD in an effort to "hear something similar" recorded in the 1930s. Clearly, though, we cannot listen to the sounds of slavery, not just because they were never recorded but also because the context in which the sounds were produced and the context in which we consume them has altered so radically.[35]

The CD itself is problematic. After all, slavery's soundscape was constituted as much by its silences, quiet moments, stealthy rustles, whispers beyond the masters' ears, and the deliberately quiet aspects of slave religion. For Shane White and Graham White, though, the barely audible is less reliable for understanding African American culture. As they put it, "slave culture was made to be heard." But it was not, at least not always, and the aural contours of slave culture were far more varied, subtle, and textured than the term "sounds of slavery" can permit.[36] The authors' privileging of slavery's audibility is in part a product of the book's format and presentation. The CD is simply full of sound because, well, it has to be. Some sounds, it seems, are more important, consumable, and marketable than others.

So why include a CD or any electromagnetic recording in such a project? I can only speculate, of course, but at work here was probably a (noble) desire to reach beyond a scholarly audience and a concomitant belief that recording technologies make sound more importable from the past and exportable to the present. I remain unconvinced. Shane White and Graham White could do no more for the smells of slavery than what they have done for the sounds of slavery. Would any historian of the senses specifically—or any historian generally—claim, for example, that it was possible to reproduce (per the common claim by slaveholders) an enslaved person's distinctive, racially determined odor? The olfactory construction—one tightly indexed to racial stereotyping in service of continued othering and subordination—was just that: a construction, a conceit, and, as such, a product of ideology. To claim to be able to reproduce and reconsume this fictional "black" scent would be tantamount to unquestioning acceptance of the slaveholders' worldview and, in effect, replicate that worldview. Little wonder, then, that no one has made such a claim. And, for the same contextual reasons, we should be wary of making the claim about sound.[37]

Indeed, other historians, especially those writing after *The Sounds of Slavery* was published, have resisted the temptation to include sound recordings in their books. Karin Bijsterveld could have easily included a CD of recordings of traffic and aircraft noise in her 2008 study *Mechanical Sound: Technology, Culture, and Public Problems of Noise in the Twentieth Century*. She could have used actual recordings and sold them, with her book, to people interested in what noise supposedly sounded like in the 1940s, '50s, and '60s. But she did not because, as her entire study shows, sounds and noises can only be understood in their historical context. Bijsterveld is aware of the seductive allure of the CD but resists its temptation on epistemological grounds: "At first sight, one might expect this study to be accompanied by a compact disk with historical recordings or contemporary recordings of historical artifacts. This, it seems to me, would not be very helpful." She explains, quite correctly: "Listening to a recording of museum steam machines might give you the impression that these machines were not very 'loud' at all, forgetting that steam machines may not have been as well-oiled when originally in use as when in use in a museum decades later." In other words, unless used with attention to context, recordings can be ahistorical and, as such, not only fail to communicate which constituencies heard what and how and why but, in fact, can and do function to lull the unwitting listener into thinking that what they are hearing is freighted with the same meaning as the sound (or silence) in its original context.[38]

There are other, pressing reasons, not to include or rely heavily on recorded sound in such a fashion. Here, we return to Jennifer Lynn Stoever's trenchant 2016 study, *The Sonic Color Line: Race and the Cultural Politics of Listening*. Stoever is expressly not interested in "recovering" the lost sounds of race and race-making. She articulates and marries "'actual' sounds with textual representations of listening and the auditory imaginary." Stoever treats sound "not as an object of study, but as a method enabling an understanding of race as an aural experience." Here, Stoever is pursuing an "acoustic archaeology," one dedicated not necessarily to reproducing sounds but, rather, learning to listen to texts—and the auditory evidence embedded in them. While the habit of understanding how sound comes to us already filtered and listened to does not preclude listening to recordings, it does inculcate the healthy and important habit of excavating and historicizing sounds from texts in an effort to understand ways of listening and hearing that are historically specific. There are, then, real dividends for historians working on sound studies in periods prior to the invention of recording technologies, especially (although not exclusively) in contexts where written texts were meant to be heard and read aloud. As Stoever puts it, "continually privileging recorded texts in the story of sound enacts a kind of technological determinism obscuring how social, cultural, and historical forces mediate sound and audio technologies." It is not the case that recordings are wholly without value, she suggests, but treating "written representations as a form of recording" allows us more readily to document and understand "the historical listening practices of the writers themselves," which, in turn, grants us access to the ways that listening habits and acoustemologies served to make race. Unwitting reliance on recorded sounds places that understanding in jeopardy; it can improperly lead us away from an understanding of embodied sound and impoverish our access to an understanding of acoustic ecologies. Moreover, it can, if not done carefully, serve to reinscribe the very stereotypes the historian seeks to interrogate by placing undue emphasis on the production of sound and the authority of the listener to define the meaning of what is heard.[39] Indeed, the most recent work by historians of sound and listening suggests we have moved on from the *Sounds of Slavery* approach. As Daniel Morat—one of the most astute scholars of historical acoustemology—has recently argued, "in sound history or the history of hearing, what is at stake is always the reconstruction of meanings that belonged, or were ascribed, to the particular sounds in question. That, in turn, can be achieved only by means of historical contextualization."[40]

Still, calls for the re-creation of the sensate, even now, are not unknown. They come primarily from living museums, the heritage industry, and other efforts to curate the senses of the past. Sensory historians play a role here and, as a result, need to think carefully about their method and their use of evidence, not least because they enjoy more ready access to public historical consciousness than many of their colleagues in other disciplines and fields. Increasingly, historians of sound specifically, and of the senses generally, are invited to advise, in a loosely curatorial fashion, museum displays and counsel the tourist and heritage industries. Political, intellectual, and market forces are at play here. The "rediscovery of the senses has become a highly profitable business," argues Robert Jütte. "Canny exhibition curators," he explains, recognize the appeal of the sensory. A number of historic homes and museums now use soundscaping to heighten the experience of visitors. Many use soundtracks to suggest the sounds of the past, and reenactors of wars—especially of the US Civil War—go to great lengths in an effort to re-create with fidelity the sounds of cannons, guns, and shells in an earnest effort to add authenticity to their re-creations of key battles.[41]

Sound, but also smell, has figured prominently in such curatorial efforts. In 1984 the York Archaeological Trust opened Jorvik, a Viking village in the United Kingdom, where patrons were invited to smell the past via the use of scratch-and-sniff cards. Not all historians are entirely dismissive of the Jorvik enterprise. Despite his reservations about Jorvik's (unwitting) reinscription of "the toilet-training theory of history—the notion that the remote past was marked by squalor and stench, and modernity by a *nostalgie de la merde*," Mark S. R. Jenner offers something of a critique of the limits of the written word's ability to capture the authenticity of the sensory past: "No matter how much historians grub around in archives and no matter how colourful and evocative the vocabulary we employ, we are not going to produce work that is as pungent as the scratch and sniff cards of the Viking privy that you can buy at the end of your trip under Coppergate."[42]

Jenner has a point, but it is one with limits. My principal objection to these sorts of curatorial tricks is that, without due attention to the critical importance of context, we wrongly marry the production of the past to its present-day consumption. While it is perfectly possible to re-create the decibel level

and tone of a hammer hitting an anvil from the nineteenth century, or a piece of music from 1750 (especially if we still have
the score and original instruments), it is impossible to experience those sensations in the same way as those who heard the
hammer or the music. What was noise, sound, comforting, or
chilling to, say, a nineteenth-century ear is not entirely recov-
erable today not least because that world—how those sounds
were perceived and understood by multiple constituencies—
has evaporated. The same holds true for all historical evidence,
visual included. For example, "we" do not "see" the engraving
of a slave whipping from the 1830s in the same light, with the
same meaning, or with the same emotional intensity or meaning as the abolitionist did at the time. That something as seemingly straightforward as a color was, in fact, subject to significant
variation not only in its meaning but in its very definition suggests the danger in making easy claims for the senses generally.
As Joy Parr argues, a full understanding of the meaning of the
senses demands not only a highly contextualized understanding of the sensory environment but a fully aware appreciation
of "historically specific bodies," bodies whose sensory appara-
tus is most accurately understood and appreciated as being in
and of a moment in time and place.[43]

Indeed, even the reproducibility of past sensations should
not be taken for granted. Can we really re-create the sounds of
eighteenth-century urban areas as with, say, Colonial Williamsburg in Virginia? What about the low rumble of jet planes over-
head and the intrusive beat of nearby traffic? Should personal
stereos be banned in such environments, lest degraded noise
from earphones spill into the soundscape of those trying anx-
iously to experience the soundscape of Williamsburg "as it once
was"? What of Civil War reenactors in the United States? Can
they really re-create battles in their full sensory texture? Acoustic shadows—accidents of climate and geography creating sounds

that appeared to come from one direction but emanated from another—were not unknown during Civil War engagements. Those conditions cannot be reproduced, and so neither can the experience of those battles where acoustic shadows occurred be reconsumed.

Museums wishing to deploy the senses need better advice, it seems to me, as does the public they serve. Sensory historians can advise curators not only on which sounds or smells or sights to deploy (either newly recorded or archivally reproduced) but also on how to deploy them, and here I think we need to stress the preeminent importance of contextualizing the senses that museum visitors experience. Rather than simply feeding sounds to ears and smells to noses, we need to help visitors understand the context in which those sounds, and smells, were produced and how their reproduction can tell us not only about the nature of the past but about our own intellectual sensory preferences and prejudices. Should we fail in that fundamental challenge, the habit of sensory history will have reverted to the sort of experiential fantasy pioneered a century ago by Huizinga.

# Notes

Introduction

1. "Sensory history" is a more commonly used term than "histories of the senses," although the latter is not without its adherents. See Jütte, *History of the Senses.* To be sure, terminologies vary within specific sensory subfields, too, as is the case with historical sound studies. See, for example, Novak and Sakakeeny, *Keywords in Sound*; Rath, *How Early America Sounded*; Sterne, *Sound Studies Reader*, esp. 13.

2. Howes, "Introduction," 1.

3. My initial foray was in the form of a debate with Mitchell Snay and Bruce Smith in 2000–2002. See M. M. Smith, "Listening to the Heard Worlds," 63–97; M. M. Smith, "Echoes in Print," 317–36. The essays and debate are most readily accessed in M. M. Smith, *Hearing History*, 365–404. Some of the points I offer here I've made in different form before. See especially my "Making Sense of Social History," 165–86; "Producing Sense," 841–58; *Sensory History*; "Getting in Touch," 381–91; "Touch of an Uncommon Man," B6; "Sound—So What?," 132–44; "Afterword: Useful Echoes," 243–48. My modest influence on some of what is published in the field is due in part to my former position as general editor of the Studies in Sensory History series published by the University of Illinois Press (2008–18) and my current general editorship of the series Perspectives in Sensory History, published by Penn State University Press.

4. The authoritative collection on the interdisciplinary nature of sensory studies is Howes, *Senses and Sensation.*

Chapter 1

1. Hilmes, "Is There a Field?," 249–59.

2. See, for example, Saab, *Objects of Vision.*

3. See, though, Graeme Wynn's excellent foreword to Joy Parr's seminal work, *Sensing Changes*, xvii–xviii; Hoffer, *Sensory Worlds*, 18. See also Hilmes, "Is There a Field?" Others have traced writing on the history of the senses to the 1980s. See Hoegaerts and Kilpiö, "Noisy Modernization?," 610–18, esp. 611.

4. For some other important influences, see Howes, "Introduction," which helpfully summarizes the important contributions of Roy Porter, the influential social historian; Sidney Mintz, the anthropologist; and several sociologists.

5. Ibid., 2; Otterspeer, *Reading Huizinga.*

6. Ankersmit, "Huizinga on Historical Experience," quotations (in order) on 24, 27, 29. On Huizinga's shift from experience to sensation,

see Howes, "Introduction," 2. On Huizinga, the senses, and emotion, see Boddice and Smith, *Emotion, Sense, Experience*, 3–5.

7. Huizinga, *Waning of the Middle Ages*, 2. On Ong and McLuhan, see M. M. Smith, *Sensory History*, esp. 8, 10–17.

8. Huizinga, *Waning of the Middle Ages*, 2. Sounds and the function of colors occupy Huizinga. See ibid., 43, 173. See also Le Goff, *Time, Work and Culture*; Boddice and Smith, *Emotion, Sense, Experience*.

9. Ankersmit, "Huizinga on Historical Experience," quotations (in order) on 24, 27, 29, 33.

10. Huizinga, "Task of Cultural History," 17–76, quotation on 26. The basis of the essay was first given as a speech in 1926 and then published in 1929 (17).

11. This list of historians working on the senses is not exhaustive. Jacques Léonard, for example, offers some useful insights in his excellent *Archives du corps*, esp. chapters 2 and 5.

12. Hunt, "French History," 209–24.

13. Febvre, *Problème de l'incroyance*. To be sure, Bloch wrote an important book on the "royal touch" but rarely attended to the sensory otherwise; Braudel, the other preeminent *Annales* School historian, leaned more heavily on economics than he did on *mentalité*. See Febvre, *Problem of Unbelief*, xxii–xxiii; Godfrey, "Alain Corbin," 381–98, esp. 397.

14. Febvre, *Problem of Unbelief*, xxv; M. M. Smith, *Sensory History*. This book was reissued by the University of California Press in 2008 as *Sensing the Past*.

15. Febvre, *Problem of Unbelief*, 423–54.

16. Ibid., 423–32, 437, quotations on 427, 432 (his emphasis). On Ong and McLuhan, see M. M. Smith, *Sensory History*, 10–15.

17. Febvre, *Problem of Unbelief*, 436.

18. Mandrou, *Modern France*, 49n1, 51. Mark S. R. Jenner's work on olfaction dutifully and helpfully acknowledged both Mandrou and Febvre, even if it was to rightly critique it. See Jenner, "Civilization and Deodorization?," 129–30.

19. Mandrou, *Modern France*, 50, 55.

20. Ibid., 50. Mandrou was on to something only recently explored by historians of religion in any detail. See Baum, *Reformation of the Senses*.

21. Mandrou, *Modern France*, 53, 54, 55.

22. Ibid., 49. On the important but underdeveloped idea of sensory habituation, see Tullett's important study *Smell in Eighteenth-Century England*.

23. Mandrou, *Modern France*, 51–52. My own early work suffered from this deficiency. See *Listening to Nineteenth-Century America*. I will say more on this matter in chapter 3, but for recent work that includes music as an important, constitutive part of the soundscape of war, see Daughtry, *Listening to War*.

24. Corbin, *Time, Desire, and Horror*, 193nn11, 13; Thuillier, *Pour une histoire du quotidien*.

25. Corbin, *History of Silence*. The book was originally published in 2016 as *Histoire du silence*.

26. Thuillier, *Pour une histoire du quotidien*, 230–32, quotations on

230, 231, 235. For his call for greater research on silence, see 239n44. The translation of Thuillier's text is my own.

27. Ibid., quotations on 232. Pinch and Bijsterveld, *Oxford Handbook of Sound Studies*.

28. See M. M. Smith, "Making Sense of Social History," 165–86; Coates, "Strange Stillness of the Past," 636–65; Smilor, "Personal Boundaries," 24–36; Smilor, "Toward an Environmental Perspective," 135–51.

29. Handlin, *Truth in History*, 227–51. On Handlin's evolution from a left wing–leaning scholar to a conservative and his prominence not only in the profession of history but in US government immigration policy, see Bailyn, "Oscar Handlin," 243–47; Bukowczyk, "Oscar Handlin's America," 7–18.

30. Handlin, *Truth in History*, 227, 229.

31. Ibid., 229, 233, 236.

32. Ibid., 241.

33. Ibid., 245.

34. Gilman, *Goethe's Touch*; Gilman, "Touch, Sexuality and Disease," 198–224. On the importance of the pioneering work of Roy Porter, work on the history of the body, and scholarship on the history of medicine to the evolution of sensory history in the 1990s and early 2000s, see M. M. Smith, *Sensory History*, 7, 32, 151n3.

35. Carter, *Sound in Between*. See also equally important work from the late 1990s in a similar vein: B. R. Smith, *Acoustic World*; Bailey, *Popular Culture and Performance*.

36. A sampling of Classen's earlier work includes Classen, "Sweet Colors, Fragrant Songs," 722–35; Classen, *Inca Cosmology*; Classen,

*Worlds of Sense*; Classen, Howes, and Synnott, *Aroma*; Classen, "Foundations," 401–12; and Classen, *Color of Angels*.

37. For Howes's work in the 1990s, see Howes, "Senses in Medicine," 125–33; Howes, *Varieties of Sensory Experience*; Howes, "Controlling Textuality," 55–73; Howes, "Scent and Sensibility," 81–89; and Howes and Lalonde, "History of Sensibilities," 125–35.

38. See Godfrey, "Alain Corbin," esp. 382–83; Gerson, "Alain Corbin," 1–117.

39. I do not include here Corbin's superb *The Lure of the Sea* not because he did not attend to the sensate in the book (he does) but because the senses played ancillary roles in the study.

40. Corbin, *Historien de sensible*, 67. See also Godfrey, "Alain Corbin," 387.

41. Corbin happily acknowledged that some of these concerns were later addressed in Thuillier's 1985 work, *Imaginaire quotidien*.

42. Corbin, *Time, Desire, and Horror*, 183.

43. Ibid., 183.

44. Roeder, "Coming to Our Senses," 1112–22, quotations on 1112, 1113, 1114.

45. Ibid., 1118–20.

Chapter 2

1. Kahn, "Sound Awake," 21–22.

2. See Reese, review of *Sounds of Modern History*, 155–57, quotation on 155.

3. The list of works on historical acoustemology alone, for example, is too extensive to note here. A good sense of its range and extent is

conveyed in Pinch and Bijsterveld, *Handbook of Sound Studies*; M. M. Smith, *Sensory History*; and the almost one-thousand-page treatment offered by Schwartz, *Making Noise*. On Asia, see McHugh, *Sandalwood and Carrion*; Low, "Theorising Sensory Cultures in Asia."

4. See M. M. Smith, "Senses in American History"; Keeling and Kun, "Sound Clash"; Jay, "Forum"; Bijsterveld, "Auditory History"; Bender, Corpis, and Walkowitz, "Sound Politics"; Bronfman and Ehrick, "Listening for History."

5. See https://www.routledge.com/The-Senses-in-Antiquity/book-series/sensesant.

6. See https://www.bloomsbury.com/uk/series/sensory-studies-series and https://www.bloomsbury.com/uk/series/sensory-formations.

7. See https://www.press.uillinois.edu/books/find_books.html?type=series&search=ssh; http://www.psupress.org/books/series/book_Series PerspectivesSensoryHistory.html; and https://www.cambridge.org/core/what-we-publish/elements/histories-of-emotions-and-the-senses.

8. See https://www.crush.group.cam.ac.uk.

9. See https://www.tandfonline.com/loi/rfss20 and http://centreforsensorystudies.org.

10. M. M. Smith, *Sensory History*, esp. 1–18.

11. Schmidt, *Hearing Things*; M. M. Smith, *Listening to Nineteenth-Century America*; Thompson, *Soundscape of Modernity*; Rath, *How Early America Sounded*.

12. For more detail, see M. M. Smith, "Renaissance Ruffs and Roman Aromas."

13. Montiglio, "Senses in Literature," 164. See also Morley, "Urban Smells and Roman Noses," 33–49.

14. See Wallis, "Medicine and the Senses," 133–52; Roodenburg, "Introduction," 1–18.

15. P. Burke, "Urban Sensations," 43–60. See also Dugan, *Ephemeral History of Perfume*; Tullett, *Smell in Eighteenth-Century England*. Carolyn Purnell's recent study of the senses in the long Enlightenment (roughly 1690 to 1830) echoes these findings. Purnell shows, courtesy of European Enlightenment intellectuals, that the sense of sight was not wholly constitutive of truth and knowledge. For example, she points out that certain aspects of eighteenth-century Parisian life diluted the importance of sight. This was, after all, a time before widespread street lighting and, as such, activities in markets were guided as much by sound and touch as by eyes that had struggled in the near-dark conditions. Purnell, *Sensational Past*.

16. Howes, *Cultural History of the Senses*.

17. Rath, *How Early America Sounded*, 104–6; Thompson, *Soundscape of Modernity*.

18. Keyes, "'Like a Roaring Lion,'" 19–43, quotations on 19–21. On noise and violence, see Attali, *Noise*.

19. What follows is an elaboration of M. M. Smith, "Welcome to Your Sensory Revolution."

20. This thumbnail sketch is developed more fully in M. M. Smith, *Sensory History*.

21. Corbin, *Foul and the Fragrant*. See also Kiechle, *Smell Detectives*.

22. Gale, "How 'Silent Spreaders.'"

23. See, for example, Bui and Badger, "Coronavirus Quieted City Noise."

24. Huber, "How Viruses Like the Coronavirus."

25. Skerritt and Shanker, "Food Rationing Confronts Shoppers."

26. Garcia, "Cómo el coronavirus destruyó." On tactility and consumerism, see Mack, "Speaking of Tomatoes," 815–42.

27. Allen, "Riots Break Out in Paris"; J. Burke, "South African Police."

28. See Parisi, *Archaeologies of Touch*; Masiello, *Senses of Democracy*, 232–57; Dave Birnbaum, *INIT: The Podcast About the Tactile Internet*, https://podcast.davebirnbaum .com.

29. An exception is Gilman, *Goethe's Touch*. But see also Chidester, "Haptics of the Heart," 61–84. For suggestive and fascinating work by a dermatologist that invites careful consideration by the historian of the senses and offers a powerful example of why historians of the senses need to engage with their colleagues in the natural sciences (and vice versa), see Shuster, "Nature and Consequence," 1–3.

30. Sullivan, *Picturing Lincoln*, 1. For an excellent treatment of Lincoln's image and its manipulation, see Holzer, Boritt, and Neely, *Lincoln Image*.

31. On the dermalogical turn, see Howes, "Skinscape," 225–39.

32. Reilly, *Abraham Lincoln's DNA*, 3–13; http://www.marfan.org /nmf/GetContentRequestHandler.do ?menu_item_id=4.

33. Finnegan, "Tactile Communication," 20–21; Bauman, *Let Your Words Be Few*, 47; "Table-Talk," 473; "Hand-Shaking."

34. *New York Herald*, February 21, 1861; Holland, *Life of Abraham Lincoln*, 263; Coggeshall, *Lincoln Memorial*, 63.

35. Sumner, *Memorial of Charles Sumner*, 159; Hutton, *Talks in a Library*, 225.

36. Gilman, "Touch, Sexuality and Disease," 202; Gilman, *Goethe's Touch*, 3, 8, 9.

37. M. M. Smith, *How Race Is Made*, chapters 1–2.

38. Elias, *Civilizing Process*, 50–56; Harvey, "Introduction," 9; Crowley, *Invention of Comfort*, 141, 142–43, 166–68. For the debate concerning the relationship between capitalism and antislavery sentiment, see the various essays in Bender, *Antislavery Debate*.

39. Burlingame, *Inner World of Abraham Lincoln*, 21–23; Huston, "Experiential Basis," 623–24.

40. Lincoln, "Fragment on Pro-slavery Theology," 204; Burlingame, *Inner World of Abraham Lincoln*, 33–34. Note, too, P. Goodman, "Manual Labor Movement," 355–88.

41. Classen, "Fingerprints," 4–13; Harvey, "Introduction"; Lincoln, "Annual Message to Congress," 52–53.

42. Grenier, "Death of President Lincoln"; "Marshall's Lincoln"; Massey, "What Many Men Accomplish," D5; *Reminiscences of Abraham Lincoln*, 312.

43. For the fuller context, see the wonderful analysis offered in Boime, *Unveiling of the National Icons*, chapter 5.

44. In order, "Addresses on the Death of Hon. Jacob Collamer," 51; Holland, *Life of Abraham Lincoln*,

542; Moss, *Annals*, 244; Tumblety,
*Narrative of Dr. Tumblety*, 13; Scovel,
"Personal Recollections of Abraham
Lincoln," 502.

45. "Books and Authors," 20.

46. Stauffer, "Daguerreotyping the National Soul," 69–107. On
elite fears of postbellum moboc-
racy, see Foner, *Politics and Ideology*,
170–75. On efforts to align Lincoln with nationalism and the tus-
sle over the ownership of his image
and meaning, see Sandage, "Marble House Divided," 135–67; Boime,
*Unveiling of the National Icons*, 268–
69; Thomas, *Lincoln Memorial and
American Life*.

47. Edwards, "New Lincoln Sculpture," 2.

48. Ibid.

49. Ibid.; Dickson, "George Grey
Barnard's Controversial Lincoln," 14.

50. "Table-Talk," 473.

51. Peterson, *Lincoln*, 58–59; Sandage, "Marble House Divided," 139–
40; *Philadelphia Press*, April 11, 1865;
McPherson, *Ordeal by Fire*, 516.

52. Stallybrass and White, "Bourgeois Perception," 289–91. Classen
and Howes, "Museum as Sensescape"; Classen, "Museum Manners,"
895–914.

53. Peterson, *Lincoln*, 212n211;
Boime, *Unveiling of the National
Icons*, 273.

54. Bryer, "Yes, D.C.'s Emancipation Memorial"; Savage, *Standing
Soldiers*; Smith, *How Race Is Made*.

Chapter 3

1. Anyone interested in the most
likely direction of sensory studies
generally would be well advised to
examine the Sensory Studies website

hosted at Concordia University. See
http://www.sensorystudies.org.

2. Howes has written much on
the topic, but see especially Howes,
"Scent, Sound and Synesthesia";
Howes, "Hearing Scents, Tasting
Sights," 161–82; Howes, "Multisensory Anthropology," 17–28. For
recent work that takes synesthesia
seriously, see McCormack, *Sculpted
Ear*; Dimova, *At the Crossroads of
the Senses*.

3. Jenner, "Civilization and
Deodorization?," esp. 143–44; Jenner,
"Follow Your Nose?," 335–51.

4. Movement in this direction
may be found in the special issue of
the *Canadian Journal of Law and
Society* edited by Howes, "Vers une
déstablisation," 173–370; Hibbits,
"Coming to Our Senses."

5. Corbin, *History of Silence*.
See also the comments in Hoegaerts
and Kilpiö, "Noisy Modernization?"
On sport, see the insightful essay by
Keys, "Senses and Emotions," 21–38.

6. Mills, "Deafness." On anosmia, see M. M. Smith, *Smelling History*, xx–xxi, 55, 160.

7. Although animal studies is
burgeoning, little has been written on
this sensory aspect. See M. M. Smith,
"All the Buzz"; Massumi, "What
Animals Teach Us," 279–90.

8. Denney et al., *Sound, Space
and Civility*.

9. Little work on the senses has
been framed around modes of production. For my thoughts on the
acoustemology of the slave and cap-
italist modes of production, see *Listening to Nineteenth-Century
America*. For a very thoughtful commentary on the value of the cultural-
and social-history approach to the

senses, see Denney, "Looking Back," esp. 608–9.

10. On McLuhan and Ong, see M. M. Smith, *Sensory History*, 1–11. On the sixth sense, various other forms of perception beyond the conventional sensorium of sight, sound, smell, taste, and touch, and its relevance under modernity, see Howes, *Sixth Sense Reader*; Fretwell, *Sensory Experiments*. See also Hui, *Psychophysical Ear*. On the post–World War II era, see Parr, *Sensing Changes*. A hint at what junior scholars of the senses are undertaking is found in Trice, "Listening to 9/11."

11. See, for example, Mack, *Sensing Chicago*; B. R. Smith, *Acoustic World*; von Hoffman, *From Gluttony to Enlightenment*; Boutin, *City of Noise*; M. M. Smith, *Listening to Nineteenth-Century America*; Mansell, *Age of Noise in Britain*; Fahmy, "Earwitness to History"; Fahmy, *Street Sounds*. See also Kheshti, "On the Threshold of the Political," 51–70. A decade ago I made a similar point concerning the need for more work in non-Western sensory history. See M. M. Smith, *Sensory History*, 129. To some extent that has been taken up and, as Fahmy's work suggests, there is more being written. This is especially the case in Latin American history, which has in very recent years blossomed in its attention to the senses. See Gautier, *Aurality*; Masiello, *Senses of Democracy*; and the very helpful overview by Andrew Kettler, "Transgressing the Body Politic." Scholars of sensory studies generally—especially those in anthropology and sociology—have been more adventurous than historians when it comes to examining non-Western societies.

12. Kettler, *Smell of Slavery*; Rotter, *Empires of the Senses*.

13. Peri, *War Within*, 47–58. See also S. Goodman, *Sonic Warfare*; M. M. Smith, *Smell of Battle*; Cornish and Saunders, *Modern Conflict and the Senses*; Das, *Touch and Intimacy*; Bruton and Gooday, "Listening in Combat," 213–26; M. M. Smith, "Krieg," 391–95. On sounds and mobilization for war, see Birdsall, *Nazi Soundscapes*, esp. 103–19; on the sensory history of war prisoners, see the pathbreaking study by Kutzler, *Living by Inches*. Little has been written on the sensory experience for World War II. What has been is excellent. See MacKenzie, "Maximizing Sensory Perception," 64–71; MacKenzie, "Sensory Stress and Personal Agency," 107–28. For the post–World War II era, even less has been written, but see Hui and Camprubí, "Testing the Underwater Ear." Revolutions, too, deserve much closer sensory scrutiny. See Plamper, "Sounds of February," 1–26.

14. On human-made disasters, see Parr, *Sensing Changes*; on the importance of recognizing the full environmental landscape in all its complexity, see M. M. Smith, "Why Historians," 67–74; M. M. Smith, "Garden in the Machine," 39–57. On the sensory history of a hurricane, see M. M. Smith, *Camille*. On the 1867 events, see M. M. Smith, "Sensorium on a Constant Strain.'"

15. M. M. Smith, "Making Sense of Social History," 165–86; M. M. Smith, "Producing Sense," 841–58.

16. Bronfman and Ehrick, "Forum Introduction," 211.

17. See Hoegaerts and Kilpiö, "Noisy Modernization?," 612, 613; Sterne, *Audible Past*, 7. See also the

astute commentary offered by Hertzman, "Toward and Against a Sounded
History," 249–58; and Hui, *Psychophysical Ear.*

18. Stoever, *Sonic Color Line*, 18.
See also Suisman, "Thinking Historically," 1–12; Botstein, "Toward a History of Listening," 427–31.

19. Daughtry, *Listening to War;*
Hammond, *Powers of Sound and
Song.*

20. M. M. Smith, *Hearing History*, 365–404; Rindisbacher, *Smell of
Books.*

21. For a full elaboration of this
argument, see Boddice and Smith,
*Emotion, Sense, Experience.* Note,
too, Boddice, "Developing Brain as
Historical Artifact." Comparatively
little historical work linking the
senses with emotion has been under-
taken. But see Hitzer, "Odor of Disgust"; Keys, "Senses and Emotions";
MacKenzie, "Sensory Stress and Personal Agency"; Denney, "The Emotions, the Senses"; Plamper, "Sounds
of February," 4.

22. On the "emerged" state of the
field of historical acoustemology and
sound studies, for example, see Stoever, *Sonic Color Line.*

23. Anthropologists have proven
rather less diffident in their critiques
of one another but not always to
profitable—or civil—effect. See, for
example, Ingold, "Worlds of Sense,"
313–17. See also Howes, "Multisensory Anthropology," esp. 22–23.

24. Corbin, *Time, Desire, and Horror*, esp. 183.

25. Jenner, "Civilization and
Deodorization?," 137–38.

26. Corbin, *Time, Desire, and Hor-
ror*, esp. 10–12; Reinarz, *Past Scents;*
Tullett, *Smell in Eighteenth-Century
England.*

27. Any discussion of touch
and taste should begin with Korsmeyer, *Making Sense of Taste;* Classen, *Deepest Sense.* For an excellent
example of how the study of taste can
tell us about not just culture but also
the nature of politics, see Bégin, *Taste
of the Nation.*

28. See Gregor's review of *Sounds
of Modern History.*

29. Kelman, "Rethinking the
Soundscape," 212–34. See also Helmreich, "Listening Against Soundscapes," 10. For an especially
thoughtful survey of work on historical acoustemology, see Birdsall, *Nazi
Soundscapes*, 21–26.

30. See, for example, Gallagher,
"Use of Sensory Language," 68–82.

31. Huizinga, "Task of Cultural
History," 39.

32. See M. M. Smith, *Smell of
Battle*, 1–5.

33. This is, of course, not to say
that sensory history can't be per-
tinent to modern concerns, as the
above discussion of the senses and
COVID-19 shows. Informative pieces
on the senses have earned coverage in
major news outlets. See, for example,
Eakin, "History You Can See"; Luhrmann, "Can't Place That Smell?";
M. M. Smith, "Abraham Lincoln,
Joe Biden." The issue, here, is the
increasingly strict tethering of funding to "relevance" or "impact." See,
for example, the Economic and Social
Research Council in the United Kingdom, which explicitly ties a "good"
research application to a "specific
impact strategy." See https://esrc.ukri
.org/funding/guidance-for-applicants
/how-to-write-a-good-research-grant
-proposal. Also note the Netherlands
Organization for Scientific Research
and "knowledge utilization," https://

www.nwo.nl/en/policies/knowledge
+utilisation. The obvious point to be
made here is that historians often
cannot reliably anticipate or imagine what the "impact" of their work
will be in either the long or short
run, while the funding mechanism
encourages them to make precisely
these sorts of claims.

34. Huizinga, "Task of Cultural
History," 41.

35. White and White, *Sounds of
Slavery*, xxi, xxii, 21, 28. The Lomax
recordings demand a much fuller discussion than the Whites offer. See
Jonathan Sterne's sophisticated ques-
tioning of "the ideology of trans-
parency suggested by ethnographic
recordists" in his 2003 study, *Audible
Past*, 319.

36. White and White, *Sounds of
Slavery*, ix.

37. M. M. Smith, *How Race Is
Made*.

38. Bijsterveld, *Mechanical
Sound*, 25. See also M. M. Smith,
"Sound—So What?," 132–44.

39. Stoever, *Sonic Color Line*, 6,
7, 18, 23, 24–25. See also Corbould,
"Streets, Sounds and Identity," 859–
94; B. R. Smith, *Acoustic World*; B. R.

Smith, "Listening to the Wild Blue
Yonder," esp. 23–24, 33; Fisher, *Music,
Piety, and Propaganda*, 7–10.

40. Morat, "Sound of a New Era,"
591–609, quotation on 592.

41. Jütte, *History of the Senses*,
1–3, 8–9. On the US Civil War, see
M. M. Smith, *Smell of Battle*.

42. Jenner, "Civilization and
Deodorization?," 128–29. Still, the
general thrust of Jenner's essay
exposes the (Jorvik) conceit that such
efforts to smell the past tend, quite
wrongly, to other that same past
and its inhabitants and inaccurately
affirm that "smell was more central
to earlier societies than our own."
See also Kiechle, "Preserving the
Unpleasant," 22–32.

43. Properly framed and contextualized, it is possible for curators
to anchor the sensory artifacts they
deploy to profile what those sensory
experiences "meant" to contemporaries. For recent thinking on museums
and sound, see Bijsterveld, "Ears-on
Exhibitions," 73–90. On color and
context, see Pastoureau, *Blue*. Parr,
*Sensing Changes*, esp. 189–91, quotation on 189.

# Bibliography

"Addresses on the Death of Hon. Jacob Collamer, Delivered in the Senate and House of Representatives, on Thursday, December 4, 1865." United States, 39th Congress, 1st session, 51. Washington, DC: Government Printing Office, 1866.

Allen, Peter. "Riots Break Out in Paris." *Daily Mail*, April 19, 2020. https://www.dailymail .co.uk/news/article-8235307 /Riots-break-suburbs-Paris -amid-anger-French-police -heavy-handedness-lockdown .html.

Ankersmit, Frank. "Huizinga on Historical Experience." In Howes, *Senses and Sensation*, 2:23–46.

Attali, Jacques. *Noise: The Political Economy of Music.* Translated by Brian Massumi. Minneapolis: University of Minnesota Press, 1985.

Bailey, Peter. *Popular Culture and Performance in the Victorian City.* Cambridge: Cambridge University Press, 1998.

Bailyn, Bernard. "Oscar Handlin." *Proceedings of the American Philosophical Society* 157 (2013): 243–47.

Baum, Jacob. *Reformation of the Senses: The Paradox of Religious Belief and Practice in Germany.* Urbana: University of Illinois Press, 2019.

Bauman, Richard. *Let Your Words Be Few: Symbolism of Speaking and Silence Among Seventeenth-Century Quakers.* Cambridge: Cambridge University Press, 1983.

Bégin, Camille. *Taste of the Nation: The New Deal's Search for America's Food.* Urbana: University of Illinois Press, 2016.

Bender, Daniel, Duane J. Corpis, and Daniel J. Walkowitz, eds. "Sound Politics: Critically Listening to the Past." Special issue, *Radical History Review* 121 (2015): 1–7.

Bender, Thomas, ed. *The Antislavery Debate: Capitalism and Abolitionism as a Problem in Historical Interpretation.* Berkeley: University of California Press, 1992.

Bijsterveld, Karin, ed. "Auditory History." *Public Historian* 37 (2015): 7–13.

———. "Ears-on Exhibitions: Sound in the History Museum." *Public Historian* 37 (2015): 73–90.

———. *Mechanical Sound: Technology, Culture, and Public Problems of Noise in the Twentieth Century.* Cambridge: MIT Press, 2008.

Birdsall, Carolyn. *Nazi Soundscapes: Sound, Technology and Urban Space in Germany, 1933–1945.* Amsterdam: Amsterdam University Press, 2012.

Boddice, Rob. "The Developing Brain as Historical Artifact." *Developmental Psychology* 55 (2019): 1994–97.

Boddice, Rob, and Mark Smith. *Emotion, Sense, Experience*. Cambridge: Cambridge University Press, 2020.

Boime, Albert. *The Unveiling of the National Icons: A Plea for Patriotic Iconoclasm in a Nationalist Era*. Cambridge: Cambridge University Press, 1987.

"Books and Authors." *Christian Union*, March 26, 1885, 20.

Botstein, Leon. "Toward a History of Listening." *Musical Quarterly* 82 (1998): 427–31.

Boutin, Aimée. *City of Noise: Sound and Nineteenth-Century Paris*. Urbana: University of Illinois Press, 2015.

Bronfman, Alejandra, and Christine Ehrick, eds. "Forum Introduction: Listening for History." Special issue, *Hispanic American Historical Review* 96 (2016): 211–15.

Bruton, Elizabeth, and Graeme Gooday. "Listening in Combat—Surveillance Technologies Beyond the Visual in the First World War." *History and Technology* 32 (2016): 213–26.

Bryer, Rebekah. "Yes, D.C.'s Emancipation Memorial Advances White Supremacy." *Washington Post*, June 25, 2020. https://www.washingtonpost.com/outlook/2020/06/25/yes-dcs-emancipation-memorial-advances-white-supremacy.

Bui, Quoctrung, and Emily Badger. "The Coronavirus Quieted City Noise. Listen to What's Left." *New York Times*, May 22, 2020. https://www.nytimes.com/interactive/2020/05/22/upshot/coronavirus-quiet-city-noise.html.

Bukowczyk, John C. "Oscar Handlin's America." *Journal of American Ethnic History* 32 (2013): 7–18.

Burke, Jason. "South African Police Fire Rubber Bullets at Shoppers Amid Lockdown." *Guardian*, March 28, 2020. https://www.theguardian.com/world/2020/mar/28/south-africa-police-rubber-bullets-shoppers-covid-19-lockdown.

Burke, Peter. "Urban Sensations." In *A Cultural History of the Senses in the Renaissance*, edited by Herman Roodenburg, 43–60. New York: Bloomsbury, 2014.

Burlingame, Michael. *The Inner World of Abraham Lincoln*. Urbana: University of Illinois Press, 1994.

Carter, Paul. *The Sound in Between: Voice, Space, Performance*. Sydney: New Endeavour / University of New South Wales Press, 1992.

Chidester, David. "Haptics of the Heart: The Sense of Touch in American Religion and Culture." *Culture and Religion* 1 (2000): 61–84.

Classen, Constance, ed. *The Book of Touch*. New York: Berg, 2005.

———. *The Color of Angels: Cosmology, Gender and the Aesthetic Imagination*. New York: Routledge, 1998.

———, ed. *A Cultural History of the Senses*. 6 vols. New York: Bloomsbury, 2014.

———. *The Deepest Sense: A Cultural History of Touch*. Urbana: University of Illinois Press, 2012.

———. "Fingerprints: Writing About Touch." In Classen, *Book of Touch*, 4–13.

———. "Foundations for an Anthropology of the Senses." *International Social Science Journal* 153 (1997): 401–12.

———. *Inca Cosmology and the Human Body*. Salt Lake City: University of Utah Press, 1993.

———. "Museum Manners: The Sensory Life of the Early Museum." *Journal of Social History* 40 (2007): 895–914.

———. "Sweet Colors, Fragrant Songs: Sensory Models of the Andes and the Amazon." *American Ethnologist* 17 (1990): 722–35.

———. *Worlds of Sense: Exploring the Senses in History and Across Cultures*. New York: Routledge, 1993.

Classen, Constance, and David Howes. "The Museum as Sensescape: Western Sensibilities and Indigenous Artefacts." In *Sensible Objects: Colonialism, Museums and Material Culture*, edited by Elizabeth Edwards, Chris Gosden, and Ruth Phillips, 199–222. New York: Berg, 2006.

Classen, Constance, David Howes, and Anthony Synnott. *Aroma: The Cultural History of Smell*. New York: Routledge, 1994.

Coates, Peter A. "The Strange Stillness of the Past: Toward an Environmental History of Sound and Noise." *Environmental History* 10 (2005): 636–65.

Coggeshall, William Turner. *Lincoln Memorial: The Journeys of Abraham Lincoln*. Columbus: Ohio State Journal, 1865.

Corbin, Alain. *The Foul and the Fragrant: Odor and the French Social Imagination*. Cambridge: Harvard University Press, 1986.

———. *Histoire du silence: De la Renaissance à nos jours*. Paris: Albin Michel, 2016.

———. *Historien du sensible: Entretiens avec Gilles Heuré*. Paris: La Découverte, 2000.

———. *A History of Silence: From the Renaissance to the Present Day*. Translated by Jean Birrell. Cambridge: Polity Press, 2018.

———. *The Lure of the Sea: The Discovery of the Seaside in the Western World, 1750–1840*. Translated by Jocelyn Phelps. Berkeley: University of California Press, 1994.

———. *Time, Desire, and Horror: Toward a History of the Senses*. Translated by Jean Birrell. Cambridge: Polity Press, 1995.

———. *Village Bells: The Culture of the Senses in the Nineteenth-Century French Countryside*. Translated by Martin Thom. New York: Columbia University Press, 1998.

Corbould, Clare. "Streets, Sounds and Identity in Interwar Harlem." *Journal of Social History* 40 (2007): 859–94.

Cornish, Paul, and Nicholas J. Saunders, eds. *Modern Conflict and* the Senses. New York: Routledge, 2017.

Crowley, John E. The Invention of Comfort: Sensibilities and Design in Early Modern Britain and Early America. Baltimore: Johns Hopkins University Press, 2001.

Das, Santanu. Touch and Intimacy in the First World War. Cambridge: Cambridge University Press, 2006.

Daughtry, J. Martin. Listening to War: Sound, Music, Trauma, and Survival in Wartime Iraq. New York: Oxford University Press, 2015.

Denney, Peter. "The Emotions, the Senses, and Popular Radical Print Culture in the 1790s: The Case of The Moral and Political Magazine." In Politics and Emotions in Romantic Periodicals, edited by Jock Macleod, William Christie, and Peter Denney, 49–72. Cham, Switzerland: Springer Nature Switzerland AG, 2019.

———. "Looking Back, Groping Forward: Rethinking Sensory History." Rethinking History: The Journal of Theory and Practice 15 (December 2011): 601–16.

Denney, Peter, Bruce Buchan, David Ellison, and Karen Crawley, eds. Sound, Space and Civility in the British World, 1700–1850. London: Routledge, 2019.

Dickson, Harold E. "George Grey Barnard's Controversial Lincoln." Art Journal 27 (1967): 12–15.

Dimova, Polina Dimcheva. At the Crossroads of the Senses: The Synesthetic Metaphor Across the Arts in European Modernism. Forthcoming.

Dugan, Holly. The Ephemeral History of Perfume: Scent and Sense in Early Modern England. Baltimore: Johns Hopkins University Press, 2011.

Eakin, Emily. "History You Can See, Hear, Smell, Touch and Taste." New York Times, December 20, 2003. https://www.nytimes.com/2003/12/20/books/think-tank-history-you-can-see-hear-smell-touch-and-taste.html.

Edwards, John. "New Lincoln Sculpture Nebraska Capitol." Lincoln Sunday Star, February 8, 1931, D2.

Elias, Norbert. The Civilizing Process: The History of Manners. Translated by Edmund Jephcott. Oxford: Blackwell, 1978.

Fahmy, Ziad. "An Earwitness to History: Street Hawkers and Their Calls in Early Twentieth Century Egypt." International Journal of Middle Eastern Studies 48 (2016): 129–34.

———. Street Sounds: Listening to Everyday Life in Modern Egypt. Stanford: Stanford University Press, 2020.

Febvre, Lucien. Le problème de l'incroyance au XVIe siècle: La religion de Rabelais. Paris: Editions Albin Michel, 1942.

———. The Problem of Unbelief in the Sixteenth Century: The Religion of Rabelais. Translated by Beatrice Gottlieb. Cambridge: Harvard University Press, 1982.

Finnegan, Ruth. "Tactile Communication." In Classen, *Book of Touch*, 18–26.

Fisher, Alexander J. *Music, Piety, and Propaganda: The Soundscape of Counter-Reformation Bavaria*. Oxford: Oxford University Press, 2014.

Foner, Eric. *Politics and Ideology in the Age of the Civil War*. New York: Oxford University Press, 1980.

Fretwell, Erica. *Sensory Experiments: Psychophysics, Race, and the Aesthetics of Feeling*. Durham: Duke University Press, 2020.

Gale, Jason. "How 'Silent Spreaders' Make Coronavirus Hard to Beat." *Bloomberg*, April 22, 2020. https://www.bloomberg.com/news/articles/2020-04-22/how-silent-spreaders-make-coronavirus-hard-to-beat-quicktake.

Gallagher, Gwynne. "The Use of Sensory Language in War Literature." *Colgate Academic Review* 8 (2010): 68–82.

Garcia, Rebeca Yanke. "Cómo el coronavirus destruyó los cinco sentidos tal y como los conocíamos desde hace siglos." *El Mundo* (Madrid), May 22, 2020. https://www.elmundo.es/papel/historias/2020/05/24/5ebe92b321efa0f9718b4624.html.

Gautier, Ana María Ochoa. *Aurality: Listening and Knowledge in Nineteenth-Century Colombia*. Durham: Duke University Press, 2014.

Gerson, Stéphane. "Alain Corbin and the Writing of History." *French Politics, Culture and Society* 22 (2004): 1–117.

Gilman, Sander. *Goethe's Touch: Touching, Sexuality, and Seeing*. New Orleans: Graduate School of Tulane University, 1988.

———. "Touch, Sexuality and Disease." In *Medicine and the Five Senses*, edited by W. F. Bynum and Roy Porter, 198–224. Cambridge: Cambridge University Press, 1993.

Godfrey, Sima. "Alain Corbin: Making Sense of French History." *French Historical Studies* 25 (2002): 381–98.

Goodman, Paul. "Manual Labor Movement and the Origins of Abolitionism." *Journal of the Early Republic* 13, no. 3 (1993): 355–88.

Goodman, Steve. *Sonic Warfare: Sound, Affect, and the Ecology of Fear*. Cambridge: MIT Press, 2012.

Gregor, Neil. Review of *Sounds of Modern History: Auditory Cultures in 19th- and 20th-Century Europe*, edited by Daniel Morat. *Sehepunkte* 15, no. 1 (2015). http://www.sehepunkte.de/2015/01/25587.html.

Grenier, Edouard. "The Death of President Lincoln." Translated by Mrs. Anne C. L. Botta. *Harper's Weekly*, October 19, 1867.

Hammond, Nicholas. *The Powers of Sound and Song in Early Modern Paris*. University Park: Pennsylvania State University Press, 2019.

Handlin, Oscar. *Truth in History*. New Brunswick, NJ: Transaction, 1998.

"Hand-Shaking." *Harper's Weekly*, May 21, 1870.

Harvey, Elizabeth D. "Introduction: The Sense of All Senses." In *Sensible Flesh: On Touch in Early Modern Culture*, edited by Elizabeth D. Harvey, 1–9. Philadelphia: University of Pennsylvania Press, 2003.

Helmreich, Stefan. "Listening Against Soundscapes." *Anthropology News* 51, no. 9 (2010): 10. https://anthro source.onlinelibrary.wiley.com /doi/abs/10.1111/j.1556-3502 .2010.51910.x.

Hertzman, Marc A. "Toward and Against a Sounded History." *Hispanic American Historical Review* 96 (2016): 249–58.

Hibbits, Bernard. "Coming to Our Senses: Communication and Legal Expression in Performance Culture." *Emory Law Journal* 41 (1992): 873–960. https://www.law.pitt.edu/ archive/hibbitts/ctos.htm.

Hilmes, Michele. "Is There a Field Called Sound Culture Studies? And Does It Matter?" *American Quarterly* 57 (2005): 249–59.

Hitzer, Bettina. "The Odor of Disgust: Contemplating the Dark Side of 20th-Century Cancer History." *Emotion Review* 2, no. 3 (2020): 156–67.

Hoegaerts, Josephine, and Kaarina Kilpiö. "Noisy Modernization? On the History and Historicization of Sound." *International Journal for History, Culture and Modernity* 7 (2019): 610–18.

Hoffer, Peter Charles. *Sensory Worlds in Early America*. Baltimore:

Johns Hopkins University Press, 2003.

Hoffman, Viktoria von. *From Gluttony to Enlightenment: The World of Taste in Early Modern Europe*. Urbana: University of Illinois Press, 2017.

Holland, J. G. *The Life of Abraham Lincoln*. Springfield, MA: Gurdon Bill, 1866.

Holzer, Harold, Gabor S. Boritt, and Mark E. Neely Jr. *The Lincoln Image: Abraham Lincoln and the Popular Print*. Urbana: University of Illinois Press, 2005.

Howes, David. "Controlling Textuality: A Call for a Return to the Senses." *Anthropologica* 33 (1990): 55–73.

———, ed. *A Cultural History of the Senses in the Modern Age*. New York: Bloomsbury, 2014.

———. "Hearing Scents, Tasting Sights: Toward a Cross-Cultural Multimodal Theory of Aesthetics." In *Art and the Senses*, edited by Francesca Bacci and David Mellon, 161–82. Oxford: Oxford University Press, 2011.

———. "Scent and Sensibility." *Culture, Medicine and Psychiatry* 13 (1989): 81–89.

———. "Scent, Sound and Synesthesia: Intersensoriality and Material Culture Theory." In *Handbook of Material Culture*, edited by Christopher Tilley, Webb Keane, Susanne Kuechler-Fogden, Mike Rowlands, and Patricia Spyer, 161–72. London: Sage, 2006. http:// sk.sagepub.com/reference /hdbk_matculture/n11.xml.

———. "The Senses in Medicine." *Culture, Medicine and Psychiatry* 19 (1995): 125–33.

———, ed. *The Sixth Sense Reader.* New York: Berg, 2009.

———. "Introduction: On the History and Sociology of the Senses." In Howes, *Senses and Sensation,* 2:1–20.

———. "Multisensory Anthropology." *Annual Review of Anthropology* 48 (2019): 17–28.

———, ed. *Senses and Sensation: Critical and Primary Sources.* 4 vols. London: Bloomsbury Academic, 2018.

———. "The Skinscape: Reflections on the Dermalogical Turn." *Body and Society* 24 (2018): 225–39.

———, ed. *The Varieties of Sensory Experience: A Sourcebook in the Anthropology of the Senses.* Toronto: University of Toronto Press, 1991.

———. "Vers une déstablisation du sensorium du droit: Étude de la jurisprudence des sens / Troubling Law's Sensorium: Explorations in Sensational Jurisprudence." Special issue, *Canadian Journal of Law and Society* 34 (2019): 173–370.

Howes, David, and Marc Lalonde. "The History of Sensibilities: Of the Standard of Taste in Mid-Eighteenth Century England and the Circulation of Smells in Post-Revolutionary France." *Dialectical Anthropology* 16 (1991): 125–35.

Huber, Jennifer. "How Viruses Like the Coronavirus Can Steal Our Sense of Smell." *Scope,* April 17, 2020. https:// scopeblog.stanford.edu/2020/04/17/how-viruses-like-the-coronavirus-can-steal-our-sense-of-smell.

Hui, Alexandra. *The Psychophysical Ear: Musical Experiments, Experimental Sounds, 1840–1910.* Cambridge: MIT Press, 2012.

Hui, Alexandra, and Lino Camprubí. "Testing the Underwater Ear: Hearing, Standardizing, and Classifying Marine Sounds During the Cold War." In *Testing Hearing: The Making of Modern Aurality,* edited by Alexandra Hui, Mara Mills, and Viktoria Tkaczyk, 371–88. New York: Oxford University Press, 2020.

Huizinga, Johan. "The Task of Cultural History." In *Men and Ideas: History, the Middle Ages, the Renaissance,* edited by Johann Huizinga, 17–76. Princeton: Princeton University Press, 1984.

———. *The Waning of the Middle Ages.* N.p.: Benediction Classics, 2009.

Hunt, Lynn. "French History in the Last Twenty Years: The Rise and Fall of the *Annales* Paradigm." *Journal of Contemporary History* 21 (1986): 209–24.

Huston, James L. "The Experiential Basis of the Northern Antislavery Impulse." *Journal of Southern History* 56 (1990): 609–40.

Hutton, Laurence. *Talks in a Library with Laurence Hutton, Recorded by Isabel Moore.* New York, 1905.

Ingold, Tim. "Worlds of Sense and Sensing the World: A Response to Sarah Punk and David Howes." *Social Anthropology / Anthropologie Sociale* 19 (2011): 313–17.

Jay, Martin, ed. "Forum: The Senses in History." *American Historical Review* 116 (2011): 207–15.

Jenner, Mark S. R. "Civilization and Deodorization? Smell in Early Modern English Culture." In *Civil Histories: Essays Presented to Sir Keith Thomas*, edited by Peter Burke, Brian Harrison, and Paul Slack, 127–44. New York: Oxford University Press, 2000.

———. "Follow Your Nose? Smell, Smelling, and Their Histories." *American Historical Review* 116, no. 2 (2011): 335–51.

Jütte, Robert. *A History of the Senses: From Antiquity to Cyberspace*. Cambridge: Polity Press, 2005.

Kahn, Douglas. "Sound Awake." *Australian Review of Books*, July 2000, 21–22.

Keeling, Kara, and Josh Kun, eds. "Sound Clash: Listening to American Studies." *American Quarterly* 63 (2011): 445–59.

Kelman, Ari Y. "Rethinking the Soundscape: A Critical Genealogy of a Key Term in Sound Studies." *Senses and Society* 5 (2010): 212–34.

Kettler, Andrew. *The Smell of Slavery: Olfactory Racism and the Atlantic World*. New York: Cambridge University Press, 2020.

———. "Transgressing the Body Politic: Perceiving Race, Gender, and God in Latin American Sensory Studies." *Senses and Society* (forthcoming).

Keyes, Sarah. "'Like a Roaring Lion': The Overland Trail as a Sonic Conquest." *Journal of American History* 96 (2009): 19–43.

Keys, Barbara. "Senses and Emotions in the History of Sport." *Journal of Sport History* 40 (2013): 21–38.

Kheshti, Roshanak. "On the Threshold of the Political: The Sonic Performativity of Rooftop Chanting in Iran." *Radical History Review* 121 (2015): 51–70.

Kiechle, Melanie A. "Preserving the Unpleasant: Sources, Methods, and Conjectures for Odors at Historic Sites." *Future Anterior: Journal of Historic Preservation, History, Theory, and Criticism* 13 (2016): 22–32.

———. *Smell Detectives: An Olfactory History of Nineteenth-Century Urban America*. Seattle: University of Washington Press, 2017.

Korsmeyer, Carolyn. *Making Sense of Taste: Food and Philosophy*. Ithaca: Cornell University Press, 1999.

Kutzler, Evan. *Living by Inches: The Smells, Sounds, Tastes, and Feeling of Captivity in Civil War Prisons*. Chapel Hill: University of North Carolina Press, 2019.

Le Goff, Jacques. *Time, Work and Culture in the Middle Ages*. Translated by Arthur Goldhammer. Chicago: University of Chicago Press, 1980.

Léonard, Jacques. *Archives du corps: La santé au XIX$^e$ siècle*. Rennes: Ouest-France, 1986.

Lincoln, Abraham. "Annual Message to Congress" (3 December 1861). In *Collected Works of Abraham Lincoln*, edited by Roy P. Basler, 5:35–53. New Brunswick: Rutgers University Press, 1953.

———. "Fragment on Pro-slavery Theology" [October 1, 1858?]. In *Collected Works of Abraham Lincoln*, edited by Roy P. Basler, 3:204. New Brunswick: Rutgers University Press, 1953.

Low, Kelvin E. Y. "Theorising Sensory Cultures in Asia: Sociohistorical Perspectives." *Asian Studies Review* 43 (2019): 1–19.

Luhrmann, T. M. "Can't Place That Smell? You Must Be American." *New York Times*, September 5, 2014. https://www.nytimes.com/2014/09/07/opinion/sunday/how-culture-shapes-our-senses.html.

Mack, Adam. *Sensing Chicago: Noisemakers, Strikebreakers, and Muckrakers*. Urbana: University of Illinois Press, 2015.

———. "Speaking of Tomatoes: Supermarkets, the Senses, and Sexual Fantasy in Modern America." *Journal of Social History* 43 (2010): 815–42.

MacKenzie, S. P. "Maximizing Sensory Perception: Watch and Battle Station Choices Aboard US Navy Submarines in the Second World War." *RUSI Journal* 164 (2019): 64–71.

———. "Sensory Stress and Personal Agency: Emotional Casualty Rates Amongst USAAF Heavy Bomber Crews Over Europe During the Second World War." *War and Society* 37 (2018): 107–28.

Mandrou, Robert. *Modern France, 1500–1640: An Essay in Historical Psychology*. Translated by R. E. Hallmark. New York: Holmes and Meier, 1976.

Mansell, James. *The Age of Noise in Britain: Hearing Modernity*. Urbana: University of Illinois Press, 2017.

"Marshall's Lincoln." *Harper's Weekly*, May 25, 1867.

Masiello, Francine. *The Senses of Democracy: Perception, Politics, and Culture in Latin America*. Austin: University of Texas Press, 2018.

Massey, R. J. "What Many Men Accomplish Despite Their Handicaps." *Atlanta Constitution*, September 14, 1902, D5.

Massumi, Brian. "What Animals Teach Us About Politics." In Howes, *Senses and Sensation*, 3:270–90.

McCormack, Ryan. *The Sculpted Ear: Aurality and Statuary in the West*. University Park: Penn State University Press, 2020.

McHugh, James. *Sandalwood and Carrion: Smell in Indian Religion and Culture*. New York: Oxford University Press, 2012.

McPherson, James. *Ordeal by Fire: The Civil War and Reconstruction*. New York: McGraw-Hill, 1982.

Mills, Mara. "Deafness." In *Keywords in Sound*, edited by David Novak and Matt Sakaeeny, 45–54. Durham: Duke University Press, 2015.

Montiglio, Silvia. "The Senses in Literature: Falling in Love in an Ancient Greek Novel." In *A Cultural History of the Senses in Antiquity*, edited by Jerry Toner, 163–82. New York: Bloomsbury, 2014.

Morat, Daniel. "The Sound of a New Era: On the Transformation of Auditory and Urban Experience in the Long Fin de Siècle, 1880–1930." *International Journal for History, Culture and Modernity* 7 (2019): 591–609.

———, ed. *Sounds of Modern History: Auditory Cultures in 19th- and 20th-Century Europe*. New York: Berghahn, 2014.

Morley, Neville. "Urban Smells and Roman Noses." In *Smell and History: A Reader*, edited by Mark M. Smith, 33–49. Morgantown: West Virginia University Press, 2019.

Moss, Rev. Lemuel. *Annals of the United States Christian Commission*. Philadelphia: J. B. Lippincott, 1868.

Novak, David, and Matt Sakakeeny, eds. *Keywords in Sound*. Durham: Duke University Press, 2015.

Otterspeer, Willem. *Reading Huizinga*. Amsterdam: Amsterdam University Press, 2010.

Parisi, David. *Archaeologies of Touch: Interfacing with Haptics from Electricity to Computing*. Minneapolis: University of Minnesota Press, 2018.

Parr, Joy. *Sensing Changes: Technologies, Environments, and the Everyday, 1953–2003*. Vancouver: UBC Press, 2010.

Pastoureau, Michel. *Blue: The History of a Color*. Princeton: Princeton University Press, 2001.

Peri, Alexis. *The War Within: Diaries from the Siege of Leningrad*. Cambridge: Harvard University Press, 2017.

Peterson, Merrill D. *Lincoln in American Memory*. New York: Oxford University Press, 1995.

Pinch, Trevor, and Karin Bijsterveld, eds. *The Oxford Handbook of Sound Studies*. New York: Oxford University Press, 2011.

Plamper, Jan. "Sounds of February, Smells of October: The Russian Revolution as Sensory Experience." *American Historical Review* 125 (2020): 1-26.

Purnell, Carolyn. *The Sensational Past: How the Enlightenment Changed the Way We Use Our Senses*. New York: Norton, 2017.

Rath, Richard Cullen. *How Early America Sounded*. Ithaca: Cornell University Press, 2003.

Reese, Henry. Review of *Sounds of Modern History: Auditory Cultures in 19th- and 20th-Century Europe*, edited by Daniel Morat. *Melbourne Historical Journal* 43 (2015): 155–57.

Reilly, Philip R. *Abraham Lincoln's DNA and Other Adventures in Genetics*. Cold Spring Harbor, NY: Cold Spring Harbor Laboratory Press, 2000.

Reinarz, Jonathan. *Past Scents: Historical Perspectives on Smell*. Urbana: University of Illinois Press, 2014.

*Reminiscences of Abraham Lincoln by Distinguished Men of His*

*Time*. New York: North American Review, 1889.

Rindisbacher, Hans J. *The Smell of Books: A Cultural-Historical Study of Olfactory Perception in Literature*. Ann Arbor: University of Michigan Press, 1992.

Roeder, George H., Jr. "Coming to Our Senses." *Journal of American History* 81 (1994): 1112–122.

Roodenburg, Herman. "Introduction: The Sensory Worlds of the Renaissance." In *A Cultural History of the Senses in the Renaissance*, edited by Herman Roodenburg, 1–18. New York: Bloomsbury, 2014.

Rotter, Andrew J. *Empires of the Senses: Bodily Encounters in Imperial India and the Philippines*. New York: Oxford University Press, 2019.

Saab, A. Joan. *Objects of Vision: Making Sense of What We See*. University Park: Penn State University Press, 2020.

Sandage, Scott A. "A Marble House Divided: The Lincoln Memorial, the Civil Rights Movement, and the Politics of Memory, 1939–1963." *Journal of American History* 80 (1993): 135–67.

Savage, Kirk. *Standing Soldiers, Kneeling Slaves: Race, War, and Monument in Nineteenth- Century America*. Princeton: Princeton University Press, 1997.

Schmidt, Leigh Eric. *Hearing Things: Religion, Illusion, and the American Enlightenment*. Cambridge: Harvard University Press, 2000.

Schwartz, Hillel. *Making Noise: From Babel to the Big Bang and Beyond*. New York: Zone Books, 2011.

Scovel, James M. "Personal Recollections of Abraham Lincoln." *Overland Monthly and Out West Magazine* 18 (1891): 502.

Shuster, Sam. "The Nature and Consequence of Karl Marx's Skin Disease." *British Journal of Dermatology* 158 (2008): 1-3.

Skerritt, Jen, and Deena Shanker. "Food Rationing Confronts Shoppers Once Spoiled for Choice." *Bloomberg*, April 21, 2020. https://www.bloomberg.com/news/articles/2020-04-21/food-rationing-is-new-reality-for-buyers-once-spoiled-for-choice.

Smilor, Raymond. "Personal Boundaries in the Urban Environment: The Legal Attack on Noise, 1865–1930." *Environmental Review* 3 (1979): 24–36.

———. "Toward an Environmental Perspective: The Anti-Noise Campaign, 1883–1932." In *Pollution and Reform in American Cities, 1870–1930*, edited by Martin V. Melosi, 135–51. Austin: University of Texas Press, 1980.

Smith, Bruce R. *The Acoustic World of Early Modern England: Attending to the O-Factor*. Chicago: University of Chicago Press, 1999.

———. "Listening to the Wild Blue Yonder: The Challenges of Acoustic Ecology." In *Hearing Cultures: Essays on Sound, Listening, and Modernity*, edited by Veit Erlmann, 23–35. Oxford: Berg, 2004.

Smith, Mark M. "Abraham Lincoln, Joe Biden and the Politics of Touch." *Salon*, April 21, 2019. https://www.salon.com /2019/04/20/abraham-lincoln -joe-biden-and-the-politics-of -touch_partner.

———. "Afterword: Useful Echoes." In *Sound, Space and Civility in the British World, 1700– 1850*, edited by Peter Denney, Bruce Buchan, David Ellison, and Karen Crawley, 243–48. London: Routledge, 2019.

———. "All the Buzz: Why Bees Mattered in the Civil War." In *Animal Histories in the Civil War Era*, edited by Earl Hess. Baton Rouge: Louisiana State University Press, forthcoming.

———. *Camille, 1969: Histories of a Hurricane*. Athens: University of Georgia Press, 2011.

———. "Echoes in Print: Method and Causation in Aural History." *Journal of the Historical Society* 2 (2002): 317–36.

———. "The Garden in the Machine: Listening to Early American Industrialization." In *The Oxford Handbook of Sound Studies*, edited by Trevor Pinch and Karin Bijsterveld, 39–57. Oxford: Oxford University Press, 2011.

———. "Getting in Touch with Slavery and Freedom." *Journal of American History* 95 (2008): 381–91.

———, ed. *Hearing History: A Reader*. Athens: University of Georgia Press, 2004.

———. *How Race Is Made: Slavery, Segregation, and the Senses*.

Chapel Hill: University of North Carolina Press, 2006.

———. "Krieg." In *Handbuch Sound*, edited by Daniel Morat and Hansjakob Ziemer, 391–95. Stuttgart: J. B. Metzler, 2018.

———. *Listening to Nineteenth-Century America*. Chapel Hill: University of North Carolina Press, 2001.

———. "Listening to the Heard Worlds of Antebellum America." *Journal of the Historical Society* 1 (2000): 63–97.

———. "Making Sense of Social History." *Journal of Social History* 37 (2003): 165–86.

———. "Producing Sense, Consuming Sense, Making Sense: Perils and Prospects for Sensory History." *Journal of Social History* 40 (2007): 841–58.

———. "Renaissance Ruffs and Roman Aromas." *Wall Street Journal*, January 30, 2015. https://www.wsj.com/articles /book-review-a-cultural-his tory-of-the-senses-edited-by -constance-classen -1422653950.

———. "The Senses in American History." *Journal of American History* 95 (2008): 378–451.

———. *Sensing the Past: Seeing, Hearing, Smelling, Tasting and Touching in History*. Berkeley: University of California Press, 2008.

———. "'The Sensorium on a Constant Strain': A Sensory History of Natural Disasters in the Danish West Indies in 1867." Danish National Archives, Copenhagen, Denmark, June 10, 2017.

———. *Sensory History*. Oxford: Berg, 2007.

———. *Smelling History: A Reader*. Morgantown: West Virginia University Press, 2019.

———. *The Smell of Battle, the Taste of Siege: A Sensory History of the Civil War*. New York: Oxford University Press, 2015.

———. "Sound—So What?" *The Public Historian* 37 (2015): 132–44.

———. "The Touch of an Uncommon Man." *Chronicle Review* 54, no. 24 (2008): B6.

———. "Welcome to Your Sensory Revolution, Thanks to the Pandemic." *Yahoo! News*, April 27, 2020. https://news .yahoo.com/welcome-sensory -revolution-thanks-pandemic -121208486.html.

———. "Why Historians of the Auditory Urban Past Might Consider Getting Their Ears Wet." In *Soundscapes of the Urban Past: Staged Sound as Mediated Cultural Heritage*, edited by Karin Bijsterveld, 67–74. Berlin: Transcript Verlag, 2013.

Stallybrass, Peter, and Allon White. "Bourgeois Perception: The Gaze and the Contaminating Touch." In Classen, *Book of Touch*, 289–91.

Stauffer, John. "Daguerreotyping the National Soul: The Portraits of Southworth and Hawes, 1843–1860." *Prospects: An Annual of American Cultural Studies* 22 (1997): 69–107.

Sterne, Jonathan. *The Audible Past: Cultural Origins of Sound Reproduction*. Durham: Duke University Press, 2003.

———, ed. *The Sound Studies Reader*. New York: Routledge, 2012.

Stoever, Jennifer Lynn. *The Sonic Color Line: Race and the Cultural Politics of Listening*. New York: New York University Press, 2016.

Suisman, David. "Thinking Historically About Sound and Sense." In *Sound in the Age of Mechanical Reproduction*, edited by David Suisman and Susan Strasser, 1–12. Philadelphia: University of Pennsylvania Press, 2010.

Sullivan, George. *Picturing Lincoln: Famous Photographs That Popularized the President*. New York: Clarion, 2000.

Sumner, Charles. *A Memorial of Charles Sumner*. Boston: Committee City Council, 1874.

"Table-Talk." *Appleton's Journal: A Magazine of General Literature* 4 (October 15, 1870): 473.

Thomas, Christopher A. *The Lincoln Memorial and American Life*. Princeton: Princeton University Press, 2002.

Thompson, Emily. *The Soundscape of Modernity: Architectural Acoustics and the Culture of Listening in America, 1900–1933*. Cambridge: MIT Press, 2002.

Thuillier, Guy. *L'imaginaire quotidien au XIXᵉ siècle*. Paris: Economica, 1985.

———. *Pour une histoire du quotidien au XIXᵉ siècle en Nivernais*. Paris: Mouton, 1977.

Trice, Allie. "Listening to 9/11: Towards an Historical Acoustemology of a Catastrophe."

BA thesis, University of South Carolina, 2020.

Tullett, William. *Smell in Eighteenth-Century England: A Social Sense*. Oxford: Oxford University Press, 2019.

Tumblety, Francis. *Narrative of Dr. Tumblety.* . . . New York, 1872.

Wallis, Faith. "Medicine and the Senses: Feeling the Pulse, Smelling the Plague, and Listening for the Cure." In *A Cultural History of the Senses in the Middle Ages*, edited by Richard G. Newhauser, 133–52. New York: Bloomsbury, 2014.

White, Shane, and Graham White. *The Sounds of Slavery: Discovering African American History Through Songs, Sermons, and Speech*. Boston: Beacon Press, 2005.

# Index

CPSIA information can be obtained
at www.ICGtesting.com
Printed in the USA
JSHW030431090721
16753JS00001B/23